THE MOUNTAIN CHANT

THE MOUNTAIN CHANT

A NAVAJO CEREMONY

Washington Matthews

Foreword by Paul Zolbrod

Orthographic Note by Robert W. Young

THE UNIVERSITY OF UTAH PRESS

SALT LAKE CITY

LIBRARY OF CONGRESS CATALOGING-IN-PUBLICATION DATA

Matthews, Washington, 1843–1905.
    The mountain chant : a navajo ceremony / Washington Matthews ;
Foreword by Paul Zolbrod ; orthographic note by Robert W. Young.
      p.   cm.
    Originally published: Washington, D.C., 1887, in U.S. Bureau of
American Ethnology, Fifth Annual report, 1883-84. With two sections
suppressed from the original edition.
    Includes bibliographical references.
    ISBN 0-87480-542-2 (acid-free paper)
    1. Mountainway (Navajo rite) 2. Navajo Indians—Rites and
Ceremonies. I. Title.
E99.N3M42 1997
299'.764—DC21   97-25249

CONTENTS

ILLUSTRATIONS

FOREWORD

BY PAUL ZOLBROD

Although much has been written about Navajo ceremonies since the initial publication of this work over a century ago, little of it has matched the intensity Washington Matthews (1843–1905) drew from the Mountain Chant as he put it into written form. And none of it registers his scope in showing how storytelling articulates a ceremonial vision of humankind's place in a broader scheme.

Scholars have recognized Navajo ceremonies as rituals of healing or blessing and often consider them discrete units. As practiced today, however, they intersect with a cohesive scheme wherein people unite with a nonhuman community that today's conventional thinking cannot yet fully accommodate. Navajos themselves see the ceremonies as a means to restore order or renew it both communally and for specific individuals. The ceremonial system is also presumed to be in decline, although it persists and may even be undergoing something of a resurgence.

Variously called dances, revival meetings, or gatherings to restore and maintain well-being, they are generally described in terms of procedure and paraphernalia rather than for what they express. In his discussion of Navajo ceremonialism in Volume 10 of the Smithsonian's definitive *Handbook of North American Indians*, for example, Leland Wyman devotes one paragraph out of twenty folio-size pages to an underlying "large body of mythology" (556). Thus the ceremonies are unevenly represented because they have drawn attention more for the objects they display and the spectacle they occasion than for any religio-poetic essence. What they express, and what their Navajo participants believe, go largely unnoticed in spite of what Matthews has recorded here.

While still practiced today, for example, the mountain chant attracts outsiders to the spectacular fire dance held on its closing night. Yet it receives virtually no attention for reiterating an episode from the Navajo storied past, preserved in a vast network of narratives that combine to identify a complex, holistic world view. Along with other ceremonies still practiced, it is valued by Navajos more as a private gathering to facilitate healing than as a public event. Days before the spectacle that serves as its climax, it attracts patients suffering from symptoms ranging from physical discomfort to debilitating states of mind. They come to summon various *diyiin din'é* or "holy people" and to reaffirm relationships beyond the human community so that health can be restored both physically and mentally.

In that regard the mountain chant resembles other ceremonies, or chantways as they are also called. And although it has been amply written about (e.g., Wyman, 1975), Washington Matthews gained an awareness of it subsequently missed by others. As someone open to how poetry and past coalesce in Navajo ceremonial practice, he managed to listen as well as watch. The result is a study both old and new that adds verbal expression to material culture and ritual action. In that context, a ceremony such as this one clarifies traditional native belief while reinvigorating Europe's literary heritage and expanding today's ecological awareness. It is my privilege to celebrate the reissue of this work by explaining why.

1

When I drive from my home in Albuquerque, as I frequently do, to the Four Corners area where the story rendered here occurred, I can see the Carrizo Mountains from as far off as sixty miles. As they come into view, I now regard them differently from how I first saw them. For that horizon is testimony to the compelling narrative that occupies the first thirty-one pages of text in this volume. My recollection of it reasserts itself—of reading it, of knowing it, of encountering it in a ceremonial setting, and of feeling in it an immediacy that does not resonate in Odysseus's homecoming, in Beowulf's return after slaying Grendel, or in any of the other great European classics that I believe this story matches for intensity and overall literary appeal.

Homer's Ithaca and all the places Odysseus passed through in returning home are far away both in time and space. The mythic Denmark of the Old English *Beowulf* likewise vanishes into an epic distance. So while ancient Ithaca or the Danish kingdom of old

Germanic lore survive in print, they cannot be seen as they appeared to those who actually sung of them. The domain in the story retold here through which the hero Dzilyi' Neiyaani or Reared Within the Mountains makes good his harrowing escape is there before me, however, just as it is visible from every direction for all Navajos. Not only does it come ever nearer as I make my way along New Mexico highway 44 across the vast expanse of Chaco Mesa. With growing vividness, I find myself recalling the story, which has become so familiar to me that it merges with the approaching horizon, as if those mountains were telling it. Literally, the terrain comes to life, thanks to the immediacy it gives the narrative, which Matthews has reconstructed so capably in written English from a vibrant oral tradition.

In a curious way, the experience reminds me of an episode in Wordsworth's *The Prelude*. There the poet recalls how as a youth he rowed a stolen skiff fervently across a moonlit lake until he spied a silhouetted promontory welling up from the dark shore. With his changing perspective the peak seemed to grow until it blocked the moon's light and he turned the boat around in the darkling water to return it, chastened, as it were, by a living landscape that all but spoke to him.

There are no roads into the Carrizos—just narrow, unimproved trails that make their high meadows inaccessible except on foot. Occasionally, I hear some elder declaring how sacred their heights are, which is why there can be never be any grading or paving in them. Once, on an afternoon in late June, a Windway singer took me up there to gather pine pollen for his ceremonies. As he gathered it in a high clearing adjoining a mountain pond, I watched lizards scurrying underfoot and birds taking wing ahead of our footsteps. The pop of grasshoppers leaping from shrubs and high blades of mountain grass followed by the buzz of their flight, merged with the whistling wind's changing pitch.

At one point I observed an owl roosting high in a ponderosa, which reminded me of the owl-masked creature's words to Dzilyi' Neiyani on the night of his escape as described in this book: "*Why don't you do something for yourself?*" Suddenly in my mind's ear there arose the exhorting chorus as first one creature then another likewise urges him onward in his arduous escape, until the distinction vanished between the words summoned from the story's recall and the wind and buzzing insects I actually heard.

Here in these mountains *The Mountain Chant* story becomes a reality—something like walking onto the stage during a dramatic production and joining the characters. Yet this is no stage but an actual place. No matter that some may now call the narrative a "myth" or a "legend" or a "folktale." The setting is real, so the story becomes real—a living part of the Navajo past that can be drawn into the present through recitation or ceremonial reenactment. By enduring in the collective memory, the story makes those mountains dynamic—teeming with discourse between humans and animals, or between the Nihokaa Din'é, or five-fingered earth surface people, and Diyiin Din'é the spirit people. With the animals they are the living source of wisdom imparted to humans in need.

That knowledge is then preserved by medicine men and other elders who reify the experience by way of the ceremony herein described. This recreates the experience of the narrative's action. Among other things, it makes me wish I could discover anew a locale for Europe's great poetry—to visit the land that furies in Aeschylus's *The Eumenides* threaten to parch; or actually listen to the "wailful choir of small gnats mourn" that Keats heard, recognizing in them autumn's doleful song. Through poetry, language and landscape can merge as a reality that was and is and will always be, adding to a powerful narrative a dimension of temporality that Europe's Great Books cannot provide a hemisphere away, however mightily they may reinvite the performing voice. Those print-inscribed words exist on the page, and their sounds may be so skillfully assembled that they can reproduce themselves in any reader's mind and be heard. But they remain incomplete with no setting where Nílch'i the wind is forever calling out advice, leaving a reader to reflect on how a ceremony might possibly add the missing dimension.

All of that comes to mind with the reading of this volume, where story and ceremony merge as a single written text. For all his presence of mind as he assembled this work, Washington Matthews very likely did not realize that by doing so he would make the Navajo landscape speak for future readers having the good fortune to visit its unchanging setting. Part of Matthews's brilliance—and I insist on calling it that, for his was the quiet, understated genius of tolerant, open-minded receptivity—was his ability to gather story, setting, repeated reenactment and overall effect into a unitary context. In so coupling the narrative and the ceremony, he brought a full sense of environment to a narrative event. Or perhaps he gave an environment an accompanying tale. Or rather he did both at once to create an ecological-poetic singularity that Navajo tradition still retains.

2

Matthews began assembling material for this work in the fall of 1884, bringing an adventurous spirit to the task. A frontier army surgeon, he had arrived in the Southwest four years earlier, having already gained notice for compiling two books on Hidatsa language and culture while Post surgeon at Fort Berthold in Dakota Territory from 1864–1867. Thereafter he served on Alcatraz Island, marched with a California expedition in pursuit of Chief Joseph, and spent a two-year tour in New York harbor.[1]

His letters make him out as a taciturn man, and his writings generally show little of a passionate side. Yet he harbored an unrelenting curiosity from the outset of his career, with a zest to know Native American life on its own terms. At Fort Berthold he sought the company of nearby Arickarees, Hidatsas, and Mandans allied against the Sioux, and listened to the lone English-speaking interpreter of Hidatsa tell the history of that tribe and recite its legends. While stationed at Alcatraz he held eighteen interviews with a Modoc leader, hoping to produce a work on that language. He readily accepted his informants as individuals, not just sources of data, and accepted Navajo medicine men as colleagues. Evidence even exists that he married the daughter of a Hidatsa chief and that she bore him a son before dying of tuberculosis. He likewise enjoyed warm personal relationships with unconventional whites whose company he sought. He conversed readily with traders, got to know some of the Dakota territory's more colorful mountain men, and made friends with noteworthy adventurers in the Southwest such as Frank Hamilton Cushing and John Gregory Bourke.

In short, the frontier he drew from was as intellectual as it was geographical. Less well noticed, perhaps, but no less important, is the literary sophistication he brought to it, predisposing him to listen in ways few Europeans ever had. While he studied cultures thought to be vanishing with a scientist's objective eye, he maintained an ear for

---

1. Marginally acknowledged for the full range of his accomplishments, Washington Matthews has gained some recognition among anthropologists and archaeologists. No book-length work on him exists, and those who have been interested in the details of his career have had to rely on Robert Poor. In production as this edition of *The Mountain Chant* goes to press, Spencer and McGreevy will be the first full volume devoted entirely to Matthews and his work.

language not only as a linguist, but with a poet's receptivity, too—as his verse translations of Navajo prayers attest. His several attempts to write poems warrant attention, especially one titled "The Eyes of Judah," which exhibits a deft allegorical skill that explains the special appeal he found in Navajo storytelling. Poetry mattered to him, and he showed boldness in recognizing that Navajos could apply it as intensely as Europe's great writers did.[2]

His comparisons of Navajo stories with elements in the Bible, Homer, Shakespeare, Milton, and Germanic and Roman mythology might seem hasty at first. But his vast knowledge of European literature—perhaps too easily overlooked—gives him unique authority to juxtapose the one tradition with the other. When he observes that he could have translated the Navajo word *hataal* as "hymnody" rather than "chant" he refers to a sequence of metrical compositions sung in honor of gods or of deified heroes—a neglected genre today. To readers as familiar with classical antiquity as Matthews apparently was, the so-called Homeric hymns come to mind, as do the songs to Orpheus and Pindar's odes.

Matthews speaks in such a vein when he makes it clear at the outset that the essential understanding of *The Mountain Chant* grows out of its underlying "myth" (paragraph 2), and goes on to explore the relationship between the underlying narrative and the sequence of chants and nonverbal activities that comprise much of the ceremony. We must be careful to understand that he applies the now-loosely-used term "myth" in a tighter classical sense, much the way Aristotle aligns it with the skillful assembly of plot in the great epics and dramas of ancient Greece. To fully appreciate what Matthews has done, then, we must remain mindful of his literary outlook rather than lapsing into today's altered perspective. With a literary awareness more common to his day than to ours, Matthews began with the right idea in suggesting that the ceremony is pivotal to the story it reenacts. Subsequent investigation has confirmed his initial insight that its basic plot gives a Navajo ceremony its cohesiveness, as this one well illustrates (see Spencer, esp. 11–50). To understand that fully, however we have to deflect attention from the ceremonial procedure itself, at least temporarily, and consider first the story that sustains it.

---

2. For the complete text of "The Eyes of Judah" and a more detailed version of this argument, see Zolbrod, 1997.

Appreciating that component is primary to a Navajo ceremony, however, and an apt way to begin to grasp the deep intricacy of Navajo creativity. Thereby we can learn to recognize fundamental poetic qualities Matthews came to appreciate once he began attending performances of the *Night Chant* and hearing elders tell of its origin. And by "poetry," I do not just mean printed lines of fixed length; I use the term more broadly to designate an art that calls attention to what it says (see Zolbrod, 1995). Its primary medium is language whether printed, spoken or sung, and may transform onto the page as prose and verse alike. Conventionally used, the term poetry draws attention more to details of sound and technique—rhyme; meter; verse structure; similes, metaphors and other tropes in isolation from the broader ideas they help to illuminate. It presupposes writing as a singular medium, removing itself from the immediacy of speech and song. As employed by Navajos along with other Native peoples whose oral traditions still flourish, however, poetry assumes broader dimensions, and richer ones, including the depth that storytelling displays in a work like this one when recognized as the ceremony's essence. Otherwise the choices that result in orchestrating such a gathering become disembodied and devoid of meaning—just as the Christmas mass would lose its much of its significance if it were to be severed from the Gospels.

Often in epic proportions, the story dwelling at the core of a Navajo healing ceremony tells of a protagonist's departure to a far-off place fraught with danger. He or she undergoes a harrowing adventure arising from heedless errors, reckless miscues, or well-intentioned but foolhardy impulses. In the story retold here, for example, Dzilyi' Neiyaani instigates his captivity by ignoring his father's admonition not to go south of the family's lodge. In other narratives the hero might be an innocent victim of neglect or abuse. She or he might be put to flight across trackless wilderness by sinister beasts or angry deities and then pushed to the brink of death by hunger, thirst, injuries or fatigue. A man is transformed into a coyote and desperately sought by members of his family; a woman captured in a deer's body is pursued by hunters. In some cases a protagonist fully perishes and must be resurrected with help from the Diyini Dine'é or Holy People—personifications of spiritual forces or natural energy (see Wyman, 1957; Luckert, 1975, 1979).

Usually appearing when all seems lost for the protagonist, they become the agents of rescue through the application of plants and herbs, specially prepared food, or carefully wrought implements, although their primary power to heal comes from the knowledge they transmit. In appearance they range from animals and insects who speak or deities who only partially materialize as masked beings otherwise scarcely described, to totally formless spirits who ride with the wind and remain unseen. It is they who administer instructions, offer advice, or orchestrate the recovery; they who train restored victims to heal their fellow mortals upon their return. That knowledge then becomes the substance and essence of the resulting ceremony, which combines the story of the original ordeal with the verbal and material components of the cure. In essence, the stories describe the acquisition of wisdom through insightful experiences and harrowing ones and usually conclude with the reunion or recon-ciliation of the returning hero with his or her mortal community. The lasting result is an intensified communal enrichment—to be pre-served by way of a ceremonial reenactment of the whole ordeal, complete with the songs and prayers that buttress the procedure.

The importance of these stories becomes evident in listening to elders who know them, not merely in examining material objects or observing procedures divorced from recitations. Considered thus, the narrative offered here invites comparison with accounts familiar to Western literary tradition ranging from the setting forth of Sir Gawain to find the Green Knight or Spenser's Redcrosse Knight to rescue Una's parents to Jane Eyre's departure from Lowwood or Holden Caufield's flight from Pennsy Prep in *Catcher in the Rye*. It deepens the significance of Odysseus's reintegration at Ithaca, or further explains Gulliver's troubled return from the country of the Houyhnhnms. It adds resonance to romantic poems of errant quest like "The Rime of the Ancient Mariner" and standard coming-of-age novels like Dickens's *Great Expectations*. It provides an important context for Tayo's predicament in Leslie Silko's *Ceremony*, and justifies calling that novel an American classic.

By opening with the narrative presented here, *The Mountain Chant* also prompts careful reflection on how return from some distant or arduous exploit is etched not only in the memory of the individual who endures it, but on how it is preserved in the common memory by one or another ceremonial procedure, whether in the form of speeches, songs, pageants or stylized retellings—reminding us all that ongoing community rests ultimately on narratives important enough to be preserved. Without that ceremonial memory, civic holidays such as Memorial Day or Veterans Day lose their relevance as benchmarks of national cohesion. Devoid of Biblical remembrances like the departure and return of the Biblical Jacob, Daniel, or Jonah, church gatherings would lose their value. The significance of ceremonial observances grows out of stories that promise to distribute ongoing comfort or pleasure to the celebrants by recreating the narrative experience of an illustrious hero forced into exile but destined somehow to return.

That, too, is a possibility Matthews apprehended. Not only is his English crisp and vivid, registering a poet's sensitive alertness to the nuances of language and capturing the story's crisp pace; it records distinctive, telltale features that make the work patently Navajo and align the *Mountain Chant* with other Native American poetic narratives and ceremonial gatherings. In doing so, he exhibits an underlying awareness of what matters to a specific culture. He accepts the growing alliance between the human protagonist and the tutelary animals and spirits at face value, for example, neither romanticizing it nor dismissing it as superstition or paganism, as earlier writers might have done. Nor does he patronize that ongoing interaction, as later translators would incline to do by treating Native American narratives as "folklore," or recreating them as children's stories. Instead he puts into the written record the Navajo essence of sacred encounters: to prevail and thrive, humans must maintain a balanced relationship with other creatures, filling out their role as stewards of a world whose balance is delicate. Godly power is far more broadly shared than it is in Homer's world, where the primary deity Zeus contends with lesser immortals to maintain his supremacy; or the Bible's world, where Yahweh goes unchallenged as the single monotheistic force, while heavenly angels function only as agents in a hierarchal chain of being. In the world represented here, though, humans, animals, and less corporeal beings form a single, interdependent community whose members address each other in terms of kinship and in effect cooperate to complete the ceremony properly, all with distinct roles to play.

In transmitting the story to English, Matthews captures its unrelenting intensity as it moves the hero through captivity, escape and return, largely by way of rapidly recursive independent clauses, with subordinate ones occurring sparingly—a technique that traditional storytellers employ to this day, facilitated by Navajo's ability to express an idea-complex in single words. Registered in his translation, for example, is the parallelism abundant throughout the narrative and intensified in the ceremony's song sequences. *"My grandchild, do something for yourself,"* the strange old woman admonishes the hero on the twelfth day of his captivity (paragraph 29). *"Why don't you do something for yourself?"* a formless creature wearing the mask of an owl hisses at him soon after darkness falls the next night (paragraph 30). Later that night he hears the familiar call of the Ye'ii Bicheii, who then warns, *"What is the matter with you, my grandchild? . . . Something you must do for yourself, or else, in the morning you will be whipped to death . . ."* (paragraph 32). And at daybreak next morning, after the hero has reluctantly stolen out of the lodge, the supernatural again appears and reiterates the warning a fourth time: *"How is it, my grandchild, that you are still here? Get on top of that spruce tree and go down into the cañon on it"* (paragraph 33).

Helped by animals large and small ranging from Mountain Sheep to Bushrat and Holy People as varied as Nílch'i the formless wind and Atsiniltl'ish the serpentine lightning, he similarly receives warnings and instructions that take on a thematic function. Issued in stylized, semirepetitive sets, those declarations produce a chorus-like effect that unites episode with episode in what becomes a cohesive story. Together they establish stylistic parallels with the song sequences that further unify story with ceremony. Read carefully, the full integration of the one with the other into a single entity becomes obvious, with the lyrics securing that unity. Recognizing these polished units of sound and syntax in the Navajo he heard, Matthews converted them to a patterned written English that illustrates a poetic awareness governing both. Words are matched with ritual activity, while symbols acquire an articulated value.

The result is a benchmark literary classic—begging first to be discovered, then explored for its depth and intricacy, and finally accepted as an essential addition to America's own pantheon of masterworks. Allowing for the inadequacy of a libretto in actually recreating the sensation of watching an opera or a musical, this text certifies a Navajo genius for incorporating dance and spectacle with social action and sacred expression. Hence it can in some ways be compared with a medieval morality play or a renaissance masque; an established opera or a Broadway musical. It provides new ways to consider the more standard Verdi and Wagner along with the newer *Jesus Christ Superstar* or *Godspell*. Fundamental to all of that, however, is Matthews's discovery that Navajo culture has something to add to America's own pantheon of great poetic works.

3

Finding himself on a boundary between a long-held literary awareness and a newly discovered oral tradition—between myth as simplistic tale and fully developed narrative poem—Matthews had no example to follow in making a ceremony a text. His published and unpublished papers demonstrate a deepening knowledge of the material and a remarkable objectivity in gathering it, but reveal little about method or personal motivation as he made his way into uncharted poetic territory. He speaks cautiously in presenting this volume, downplaying anything it might do to challenge conventional wisdom about Indians. He observes, for example, that "since the Americans, as a rule, regard all Indian ceremonies as merely dances and call them dances, I will, out of deference to a national prejudice, frequently refer to the ceremony as a dance" (paragraph 3). But he neither insists why he should record it in the first place, nor explains how he did so, calling attention to the material and not himself, unlike his friend and colleague Frank Cushing—much more the exhibitionist in putting Zuni material on the page.

Thus, little can be said about how precisely this manuscript grew or came to be published. I assume that Matthews's friend John Wesley Powell, recently appointed director of the Bureau of American Ethnology, encouraged him to assemble it—not as a literary text but as ethnological data. Nor does the ever-reticent Matthews dwell on the problems he faced. Certainly the difficulties of preparing a work like this one for a reading public must have been considerable. With no precedent to follow, he had to devise rules as he went along. He could not describe the ceremonial procedure without first acquiring specific details by watching and listening over and over, which meant night-long vigils in unfamiliar places; taking notes surreptitiously or in haste, or else struggling to memorize until things could be written down later; learning by ear alone a language as yet unwritten whose sounds and structure differed wildly from those of English and other Indo-European tongues; and all the while maintaining an openness to properties of poetry in discourse that others either dismissed or treated as data (see Faris, p. 75).

Added to such logistical and methodological problems, Matthews faced unprecedented ethical matters and social constraints. Not only did he have to decide how to acquire his material, translate it, and mount it on the page, he had to think about presenting it fairly and sympathetically to a public indifferent to Navajo culture, if not abjectly hostile. Navajo reaction itself had to be weighed, which required making hard decisions he scarcely mentions in his published work, but evidently thought through carefully. There was the issue of disclosure, for example, which he mentions privately. In a letter he later sent to someone wishing to borrow a copy of *The Mountain Chant*, he admitted that he had "been guilty of a great breach of confidence in publishing this information" (Poor, p. 32). Comments scattered elsewhere among his papers show an awareness of making other sensitive choices—including some that he may have come to regret, given the respect he developed for Navajo storytelling, song and prayer.[3]

In addition to thinking of his Navajo sources, Matthews had white sensibilities to contend with. Although originally intended for publication in a government report to specialists, it evidently contained portions that had the capacity to offend even them. Excised from the 1884 version—but included as an addendum in this

---

3. Here is the statement in its full context: "Please take special care of 'The Mountain Chant.' I send this to you by registered mail. When you have done with it, return it to me and in the mean time keep it under lock and key and let no one see it except your trusted associates in the mission work. I have been guilty of a great breach of confidence in publishing this information. Certainly when I wrote the work, twelve or thirteen years ago, it would have greatly incensed the Indians, and forever closed to me the door of knowledge had they learned of my act. Perhaps their notions have changed since that time; but there are still many conservative men among them, and they should be kept in ignorance of this work. The ordinary white men, on the reservation, who are in constant communication with the Indians, are not to be trusted either." Washington Matthews to Anselm Weber, October 1, 1898 (quoted in Poor, 32. See also 78, n. 49).

After rereading the above, I had to pause and myself reconsider whether to sanction the reissue of this text, until several colleagues and a number of Navajo elders reassured me. The book was published in 1884 by the Bureau of American Ethnology, reprinted in 1970 by the Rio Grande Press, and thus available to readers for over a century. In the meantime, a number of other ceremonies have been made available in books, some by Navajo Community College Press. Print has become an accepted means of preservation useful to Navajos and non-Navajos alike. Meanwhile, practicing medicine men still manage to withhold certain esoteric material from what they agree to release to scholars, so that highly sacred information remains uncompromised. While members of a more activist middle generation of Navajos sometimes voice objections to seeing such disclosure, more knowledgeable elders tend to embrace printed accounts of the old traditions, lest they are lost forever to youngsters who show no early interest but may wish to turn to them later.

edition—were two passages of sexually explicit burlesque included in the original manuscript. Originally following paragraph 130, one describes an imitation of canine coitus during the first dance of the ceremony's ninth night. The second, dramatizing a human couple reconciling their jealous quarrel by enjoying sexual contact, was to have followed paragraph 145 during the ninth dance that same night.

Exactly who censored the manuscript remains unknown, whereas it is easy to imagine why that was done during that time. On record, however, is one scholar's objection to the deletion. And Matthews quietly demurs by mentioning "scenes in this drama which may not be told," along with "other parts" that "have not been allowed to appear in this essay," adding with apparent irony that "recognized scientists may learn of them by addressing the author through the Director of the Bureau of Ethnology" (paragraphs 145, 146). The passages obviously belong, however, and one hopes that readers today would more generally agree with Louis Henri Aymé—the individual who took offense at the deletion back then—that the excised passages "should have been allowed to appear printed in one of our government reports," since they "are made for the purpose of spreading abroad knowledge of things of interest and importance" (cited in Poor).

Beyond suggesting that the clownish behavior in the excised passages fixes boundaries of civil behavior by breaking them, I leave it to others to interpret that portion of the ceremony. The larger issue is the wide gap that still divides print culture and oral cultures. If reproducing it was a problem for someone publishing at a time when Victorian repression was a norm, it no longer is. All the same, the incident shows that Matthews stood virtually alone on another kind of frontier—a literary frontier, you might say—where what an earlier visitor to a Navajo gathering called a disagreeable "succession of grunts" turned out to be a dramatic recreation of a mighty narrative (Letherman, 194), wherein mortals fit into a larger community of animals and spirits which animate the landscape and make the whole world a single macroorganism.

Only a relative handful of investigators by then had been willing to explore Native American thought on its own terms with the objectivity and respect Matthews displays. Fewer still managed to listen to Native voices with such literary sophistication. And none that I know of so recognized the poetic confluence of ritual and narrative. For him, attending a ceremony was not a laboratory exercise where deep poetry was transmuted to shallow data. Writing about ceremonialism was not theoretical speculation, but first-hand testimony to the poetic flowering of performance and replicating it as well as print might allow. As the material presented here demonstrates, Matthews alone, in other words, tapped Native soil to find much the same roots by which Homer and Shakespeare and Milton blossom perennially through the enduring medium of print.

Even today he stands ahead of the times. Some critics might resist his achievement on the premise that as an army surgeon he inevitably reported with a colonial bias. Along with his field notes, however, his published writings testify to a clear-headed effort to accept what he witnessed with exemplary open-mindedness. What he sensed still awaits full appreciation. For all the revisionism in how so-called Old World peoples now regard them, an awareness that Native Americans, too, possess a poetic wellspring is only beginning to register. Over a hundred years ago Washington Matthews trod a poetic frontier that readers and critics today have scarcely begun to explore. In helping to lead the twentieth century into modernism, the expatriates Ezra Pound and T. S. Eliot had to leave North American soil to elevate so-called primitivism to a classic level and incorporate it into their art. Meanwhile, poetry remains handmaiden to print, attributed to a certain hauteur still not accorded the likes of Navajo and Apache, Cherokee and Lakota, Chippewa and Iroquois. For that reason alone, it seems reasonable to produce a new edition of this work and expand its application beyond ethnology.

4

Once as I watched preparations being made for a Windway ceremony sandpainting—which also grows out of a story of departure and return reenacted to restore well-being—I spied a cricket. As if out of nowhere, it materialized on the west side of the hogan, near where the medicine man sat singing, rattle in hand. Inside were six or so people, ready to fetch sand, sift pigments, and apply tint through thumb and forefinger under his deft supervision. First he would have to determine what drawing could summon the holy people needed to meet the patient's problem. It was a solemn event, but withal a happy one, animated by activity enough to keep such a creature away. Yet it slowly approached the medicine man, as if from the insect world that Navajo stories tell of, and sat there listening until the singing ended. There it remained as the medicine man went on to diagnose the patient's malaise and explain what to draw on the hogan floor. Only then did the insect turn and move slowly out of view, as if satisfied that the proper painting would now be made and the ceremony could successfully begin.

I speak of such events cautiously, not only because my own Western skepticism makes me wonder in retrospect if they really happened, but because the skepticism of others threatens to make my account seem too fanciful to be believed. But then I think of Matthews and how he managed to overcome his European resistance and fairly represent one culture's poetic depth in full ceremonial terms. Among a people then despised either with open hostility or tacit dismissal, he found poetry at its very wellspring and had the courage to share his discovery with an audience as yet unprepared to listen or to look.

Now comes the time for hearing and seeing with full acceptance —for hastening the rapprochement between literature and anthropology; for opening up new avenues of interpreting culture and theorizing about textuality; for deepening an awareness of the interplay between human discourse and nature's own modes of expression; for redefining the sacred in terms of deep ecology. In short, the rediscovery of this text should establish Navajo ceremonialism as a source of fruitful investigation and greater understanding, along with pure appreciation for humanistic achievement. And with that acceptance should come the recognition of a poetic tradition emanating from a purportedly New World that promises to reinvigorate the established classical heritage of one only ostensibly Old.

REFERENCES

Faris, James C. 1997. "Some Observations on the Ethical Integrity of Washington Matthews in Navajo Research," in Halpern and McGreevy, 72–81.

Halpern, Katherine Spencer, and Susan Brown McGreevy, eds. 1997. *Washington Matthews: Studies of Navajo Culture 1880–1894*. Albuquerque: University of New Mexico Press.

Halpern, Katherine Spencer, Mary E. Holt, and Susan Brown McGreevy. 1985. *Guide to the Microfilm Edition of the Washington Matthews Papers*. Albuquerque: University of New Mexico Press.

Letherman, Jonathan. 1886. "A Sketch of the Navajo Tribe of Indians, Territory of New Mexico," *First Smithsonian Report*, 283–97.

Luckert, Karl W. 1975. *The Navajo Hunter Tradition*. Tucson: University of Arizona Press.

Luckert, Karl W. 1979. *Coyoteway: A Navajo Holyway Healing Ceremonial*. Flagstaff: Museum of Northern Arizona Press.

Poor, Robert Marshall. 1975. *Washington Matthews: An Intellectual Biography*. M.A. Thesis, University of Nevada Reno.

Spencer, Katherine. 1957. *Mythology and Values: An Analysis of Navajo Chantway Myths*. Philadelphia: American Folklore Society.

Wyman, Leland C., ed. 1957. *Beautyway: A Navajo Ceremonial*. New York: Pantheon Books.

Wyman, Leland C. 1975. *The Mountainway of the Navajo*. Tucson: University of Arizona Press.

Zolbrod, Paul G. 1995. *Reading the Voice: Native American Poetry on the Written Page*. Salt Lake City: University of Utah Press.

Zolbrod, Paul G. 1997. "Washington Matthews Writes a Ballad: The Anthropologist as Poet and Literary Scholar," in Halpern and McGreevy, 103–24.

NOTE ON THE ORTHOGRAPHY OF NAVAJO WORDS

WASHINGTON MATTHEWS

The spelling of Navajo words in this paper is in accordance with the alphabet of the Bureau of Ethnology:

c = *ch* in *chin*

ŧ = *th* in *this*

ç = *th* in *think*

j = *z* in *azure*

q = German *ch* in *machen*

‘ shows that a vowel is aspirated

the vowels have the continental sounds

ai is the only dipthong, and is like *i* in *line*

l is usually aspirated

the other letters have the ordinary English pronunciation

ORTHOGRAPHIC NOTE

ROBERT W. YOUNG

The orthography used for the transcription of Navajo terms in *The Mountain Chant* differs substantially from that used by Dr. Matthews in *The Night Chant* and in *Navajo Legends*. The system employed in *The Mountain Chant* is described as "in accordance with the alphabet of the Bureau of Ethnology."

The "Note on the Orthography of Navajo words" that appears on page xxiii is misleading. *C* represents *sh*, not *ch*; *Ç* represents Navajo *d* (the deaspirated *t* of *stop*), not *th* in *this*; *Ç* represents strongly aspirated Navajo *t*, not the *th* of *th*ink; and *ʿ* most commonly represents a glottal stop in the Matthews alphabet. Italic *l* was used in other texts to represent unvoiced *l*, but in *The Mountain Chant*, *l* represents both voiced and unvoiced *l* (= ł in the Modern Orthography).

The contrasting features of vowel length (= short/long duration), oral/nasoral production and inherent low/high voice pitch (tone) serve to distinguish meaning in Navajo. In the Modern Orthography long vowels are written as doublets; nasoral vowels are written with a "nasal hook" ˛ and high tone is marked with an acute accent ´. Thus:

    bitse´   = his stone
    bitsee´ = its tail
    shí   = I
    shį   = summer
    ni   = you
    ní   = he says

These distinctive features are unmarked in *The Mountain Chant*. The vowels are simply written a, e, i, o, u. (Occasionally nasality is marked by a superscript ⁿ, as in koⁿ = kǫ', fire.)

Grave ˋ and acute ´ accent marks appear frequently over vowels, but the purpose is not clear. And a dieresis indicates that two adjacent vowels are pronounced separately—usually representing a glottal stop (as in gloï = dlǫ́'ii, weasel).

The table below lists the letters of the Matthews Navajo alphabet, as used in *The Mountain Chant*, followed by the corresponding letters used in the Modern Standard Navajo Orthography; and these are followed in turn by the nearest English equivalent, if any.

THE VOWELS

Matthews	Modern Standard	English Equivalent
a	a	a (in father)
	(á, aa, áá, ą, ą́, ąą,ą́ą́)	
e	e	e (in met)
	(é, ee, éé, ę, ę́, ęę, ę́ę́)	
i	i	i (in bit/machine)
	(í, ii, íí, į, į́, įį,į́į́)	
o	o	o (in tote)
	(ó, oo, óó, ǫ, ǫ́, ǫǫ, ǫ́ǫ́)	
u	o	oo (in book)
ai	ai	i (in line

THE CONSONANTS

Matthews	Modern Standard	English Equivalent
b/p	b	p (in spot)
tc	ch	ch (in church)
*tc	ch'	— (glottalized ch)
₵	d	t (in stop)
*gl, tl	dl	— (l articulated from a d-position)
ds	dz	dz (in adze)
k, g	g	k (in skip)
*g, y	gh, y	— (a voiced velar spirant)
h	h	h (in hah)
*q	h, x	— (strongly aspirated velar spirant, something approximating the German *ch*)
dj	j	j (in judge)
*c	'	— (glottal stop, like the hiatus separating the components of the interjection "oh oh!")
k	k	k (in kill)
*k	k'	— (glottalized k)

Matthews	Modern Standard	English Equivalent
l	l	l (in low)
*l	ł	— (voiceless l)
m	m	m (in man)
n	n	n (in no)
s	s	s (in so)
C	sh	sh (in shin)
z	z	z (in zip)
j	zh	s (in pleasure)
*Ç	t	— (a strongly aspirated t)
*Ç	t'	— (glottalized t)
ts	ts	ts (in hits)
ts	ts'	— (glottalized ts)
*kl, tl	tł	— (ł articulated from a t-position)
*tl	tł'	— (glottalized tł)
w	w	w (in win)
y	y	y (in yes)

*With few exceptions, Navajo sounds identified with English "near equivalents" are approximations, and those marked with an asterisk have no near equivalent in English.

The glottal stop is not used to distinguish meaning in English, but it occurs in interjections such as "oh oh" (= o'o). It has frequent occurrence in Navajo, even as a component in the articulation of "glottalized" consonants: ch', k', t', tł', ts', for which there is no approximate equivalent in English.

G in Matthews (gh in Modern Standard) represents a "growling" sound made by raising the back of the tongue to the velar area accompained by voicing. Matthews hogán = hooghan, hogan.

Voiceless l (= ł) is produced by articulating an l-sound without voicing. Ł relates to L as S relates to Z.

SMITHSONIAN INSTITUTION——BUREAU OF ETHNOLOGY.

THE MOUNTAIN CHANT:

A NAVAJO CEREMONY.

BY

Dr. WASHINGTON MATTHEWS, U. S. A.

THE MOUNTAIN CHANT: A NAVAJO CEREMONY.

BY DR. WASHINGTON MATTHEWS, U. S. A.

INTRODUCTION.

1. The ceremony of dsilyídje qaçàl, or mountain chant — literally, chant towards (a place) within the mountains — is one of a large number practiced by the shamans, or medicine men, of the Navajo tribe. I have selected it as the first of those to be described, because I have witnessed it the most frequently, because it is the most interesting to the Caucasian spectator, and because it is the best known to the whites who visit and reside in and around the Navajo country. Its chief interest to the stranger lies in the various public performances of the last night. Like other great rites of the shamans, it has its secret ceremonies of many days' duration in the medicine lodge; but, unlike the others, it ends with a varied show in the open air, which all are invited to witness. Another ceremony which I have attended, and which the whites usually call the "Yaỳbichy Dance" (Yèbitcai), has a final public exhibition which occupies the whole night, but it is unvaried. Few Europeans can be found who have remained awake later than midnight to watch it. Such is not the case with the rite now to be described. Here the white man is rarely the first to leave at dawn.

2. The appropriateness of the name dsilyídje or tsilgitce — towards (a place) within the mountains — will be better understood from the myth than from any brief description. "Dsilyi'" may well allude to mountains in general or to the Carrizo Mountains in particular, to the place in the mountains (paragraphs 9 and 38) where the origmator of these ceremonies (whom I often find it convenient to call "prophet") dwelt, or to the name of the prophet (par. 41), or to all these combined. Qaçàl signifies a sacred song or a collection of sacred songs. From the many English synonyms for song I have selected the word chant to translate qaçàl. In its usual signification hymnody may be its more exact equivalent, but it is a less convenient term than chant. The shaman, or medicine man, who is master of ceremonies, is known as qaçàli or chanter — el cantador, the Mexicans call him. In order to keep in mind his relationship to similar functionaries in other tribes I shall, from time to time, allude to him as the priest, the shaman, or the medicine man, following

3

the example of other authors. To all ceremonies of a character similar to this the term qaçàl is applicable. It would seem from this that the Navajo regard the song as the chief part of the ceremony, but since the Americans, as a rule, regard all Indian ceremonies as merely dances and call them dances, I will, out of deference to a national prejudice, frequently refer to the ceremony as a dance.

3. Sometimes the collective rites and amusements of the last night are spoken of as ilnasjíngo qaçàl, or chant in the dark circle of branches, from *il*, branches of a tree; *nas*, surrounding, encircling; *jin*, dark; and *go*, in. The name alludes to the great fence of piñon branches, erected after sunset on the last night, to receive the guests and performers. I shall often refer to this inclosure as the corral. Some white men call the rites I describe the "corral dance," but more usually they call them the " hoshkàwn dance," from one of the minor performances of the last night, the hackàn-inçá', or act of the *Yucca baccata*, a rite or drama which seems to particularly excite the Caucasian interest. To such minor acts the terms inçá' and alìli are applied; these may be translated dance, show, act, or exhibition.

4. The purposes of the ceremony are various. Its ostensible reason for existence is to cure disease; but it is made the occasion for invoking the unseen powers in behalf of the people at large for various purposes, particularly for good crops and abundant rains. It would appear that it is also designed to perpetuate their religious symbolism. Some of the shows of the last night are undoubtedly intended to be dramatic and entertaining as well as religious, while the merely social element of the whole affair is obvious. It is an occasion when the people gather to have a jolly time. The patient pays the expenses and, probably in addition to the favor and help of the gods and the praise of the priesthood, hopes to obtain social distinction for his liberality.

5. This, like other great rites of the Navajo, is of nine days' duration. Some of these rites may take place in the summer; but the great majority of them, including this dsilyídje qaçàl, may be celebrated only in the winter, in the season when the thunder is silent and the rattlesnakes are hibernating. Were they to tell of their chief gods or relate their myths of the ancient days at any other time, death from lightning or snake-bite would, they believe, be their early fate.

6. While in New Mexico I sometimes employed a very liberal minded Navajo, named Juan, as a guide and informant. He had spent many years among Americans, Mormons, and Mexicans, and was, I imagined, almost perfectly emancipated from his "early bias." He spoke both English and Spanish fairly. On one occasion, during the month of August, in the height of the rainy season, I had him in my study conversing with him. In an unguarded moment, on his part, I led him into a discussion about the gods of his people, and neither of us had noticed a heavy storm coming over the crest of the Zuñi Mountains, close by. We were just talking of Estsánatlehi, the goddess of the west, when

the house was shaken by a terrific peal of thunder. He rose at once, pale and evidently agitated, and, whispering hoarsely, "Wait till Christmas; they are angry," he hurried away. I have seen many such evidences of the deep influence of this superstition on them.

7. When the man (or the woman) who gives the entertainment concludes he is sick and that he can afford to call a shaman, it is not the latter who decides what particular rites are best suited to cure the malady. It is the patient and his friends who determine this. Then they send for a man who is known to be skilled in performing the desired rites, and it is his province merely to do the work required of him.

8. Before beginning to describe the ceremonies it will be well to relate the myth accounting for their origin.

MYTH OF THE ORIGIN OF DSILYÍDJE QAÇÀL.

9. Many years ago, in the neighborhood of Dsilyi'-qojòni, in the Carrizo Mountains, dwelt a family of six: the father, the mother, two sons, and two daughters. They did not live all the time in one locality, but moved from place to place in the neighborhood. The young men hunted rabbits and wood rats, for it was on such small animals that they all subsisted. The girls spent their time gathering various wild edible seeds.

10. After a time they went to a place called Tse'-biçàï (the Wings of the Rock or Winged Rock), which lies to the east of the Carrizo Mountains, on a plain. When they first encamped there was no water in the vicinity and the elder brother went out to see if he could find some. He observed from the camp a little sandy hillock, covered with some vegetation, and he determined to see what sort of plants grew there. Arrived there, he noticed a spot where the ground was moist. He got his digging stick and proceeded to make a hole in the ground. He had not dug long when the water suddenly burst forth in great abundance and soon filled the excavation he had made. He hastened back to the camp and announced his success. When they left the Carrizo Mountains it was their intention to go to Çepéntsa, the La Plata Mountains, to hunt for food, and their halt at Tse'-biçàï was designed to be temporary only; but, now that they had found abundance of water, the elder brother counseled them not to hasten on, but to remain where they were for a while. The spring he developed still exists and is known to the Navajo as Çobinàkis, or the One-Eyed Water.

11. The spring was some distance from the camp, and they had but one wicker water bottle; so the woman, to lighten her labor, proposed that they should move their goods to the vicinity of the spring, as it was her task to draw the water. But the old man counseled that they should remain where they were, as materials for building were close at hand and it was his duty to erect the hut. They argued long about it; but at length the woman prevailed, and they carried all their property

down close to the spring. The elder son suggested that it would be well to dig into the soft sandy soil, in order to have a good shelter; so the old man selected a sandy hillock, overgrown with grease-wood, and excavated it near one edge, digging straight down, so as to have a wall on one side.

12. They had a stone ax-head, with a groove in it. Around this they bent a flexible twig of oak and tied it with the fibers of the yucca, and thus they made a handle. The first day after the spring was found the young men went out and chopped all day, and in the evening brought home four poles, and while they were gone the old man dug in the hillock. The next day the young men chopped all day, and at night returned with four more poles, while their father continued his digging. They worked thus for four days, and the lodge was finished. They made mats of hay to lie on and a mat of the same material to hang in the doorway. They made mats of fine cedar bark with which to cover themselves in bed, for in those days the Navajo did not weave blankets such as they make now. The soles of their moccasins were made of hay and the uppers of yucca fibers. The young men were obliged to go hunting every day; it was only with great labor they could keep the house supplied with meat; for, as has been said, they lived mostly on small animals, such as could be caught in fall traps. These traps they set at night near the burrows, and they slept close to the traps when the latter were set far from home. They hunted thus for four days after the house was finished, while their sisters scoured all the country round in search of seeds.

13. With all their work they found it hard to make a living in this place. The land was barren; even rats and prairie dogs were scarce, and the seed bearing plants were few. At the end of the fourth day they held a consultation, and the old man said they would do better to move on to the San Juan River, where food was more abundant, and they could trap and gather seeds as they traveled. They determined to leave, and next morning broke camp. They journeyed on till they reached the banks of the San Juan. Here they found abundance of tciltcin (fruit of *Rhus aromatica*) and of grass seeds, and they encamped beside the river at night.

14. Next day they traveled up the stream to a place called Tse'çqàka, and here again they halted for the night. This place is noted for its deposits of native salt. The travelers cut some out from under a great rock and filled with it their bags, made out of the skins of the squirrels and other small animals which they had captured. Thence they followed up the river to Tse'ɇezá' (Rock Sticking Up), and thence to Çisyà-qojòni (Beautiful Under the Cottonwoods), where they remained a day and killed two rabbits. These they skinned, disemboweled, crushed between two stones, bones and all, so that nothing might be lost, put them into an earthen pot to boil, and when they were sufficiently cooked they added some powdered seeds to make a thick soup; of all this they

made a hearty meal. The Navajo then had neither horses nor asses; they could not carry stone metates when they traveled, as they do now; they ground their seeds with such stones as they could find anywhere. The old man advised that they should cross the river at this point and he directed his sons to go to the river and look for a ford. After a time they returned and related that they had found a place where the stream was mostly knee deep, and where, in the deepest part, it did not come above their hips, and they thought all would be able to cross there. The father named the hour of bihilçòhigi (when it gets warm, i. e., about 10 a. m.), on the morrow, as the time they should ford the San Juan; so next morning at the appointed time they crossed. They traveled up the north bank until they came to a small affluent whose source was in Ȼepéntsa. Here they left the main river and followed the branch until night approached, when they made camp.

15. They moved on next day and came close to Ȼepéntsa, to a soil covered with tracks of deer and of other great animals of the chase. Here they encamped, and on the following morning the young men set out by different ways in the direction of the mountain to hunt; but at night they returned empty handed. Thus they hunted four days unsuccessfully. Every day while his sons were gone the old man busied himself cutting down saplings with his stone ax and building a house, and the daughters gathered seeds, which constituted the only food of the family. As the saplings were abundant and close to the camp, the old man built his house fast, and had it finished at nightfall on the fourth day, when his sons returned from their fruitless labors. They entered the lodge and sat down. They were weary and hungry and their bodies were badly torn by the thorns and thick copse of the mountains. Their father spoke not a word to them as they entered; he did not even look at them; he seemed to be lost in deep contemplation; so the young men said nothing, and all were silent. At length the old man looked up and broke the silence, saying, "Aqalàni cactcini!" (Welcome, my children.) "Again you have returned to the lodge without food. What does it avail that you go out every day to hunt when you bring home nothing? You kill nothing because you know nothing. If you had knowledge you would be successful. I pity you." The young men made no reply, but lay down and went to sleep.

16. At dawn the old man woke them and said: " Go out, my children, and build a sweat-house, and make a fire to heat stones for the bath, and build the sweat-house only as I will tell you. Make the frame of four different kinds of wood. Put kaç (juniper) in the east, tse'isçázi (mountain mahogany) in the south, ȼestsìⁿ (piñon) in the west, and awètsal (cliff rose) in the north; join them together at the top and cover them with any shrubs you choose. Get two small forked sticks, the length of the forearm, to pass the hot stones into the sweat-house, and one long stick to poke the stones out of the fire, and let all these sticks be such as have their bark abraded by the antlers of the deer. Take

of all the plants on which the deer most like to browse and spread them on the floor of the sweat-house, that we may sit on them." So they built the lodge as he directed, and lit the fire and heated the stones. While they were transferring the hot stones from the fire to the lodge the old man brought out the mats which they used for bedding, and when all the stones had been put in he hung the mats, one on top of another, over the doorway. This done the three men went into the sudatory and sat down to sweat, uttering not a word. When they had perspired sufficiently they came out and sat down in silence until they were again ready to submit themselves to the heat. In this way they sweated themselves four times, keeping all the time a perfect silence, until they emerged for the last time, when the old man directed his daughters to dig some soap root and make a lather. In this he bade his sons wash their hair and the entire surface of their bodies well. When they were thoroughly cleansed, he sent them out to set twelve stone fall traps, a task which occupied all the rest of the day. For each trap they buried a flat stone with its upper side on a level with the surface of the ground; on this they sprinkled a little earth, so that the rat would suspect nothing; over this they placed another flat stone, leaning at an angle and supported by a slender stick, to which were attached berries of the aromatic sumac as a bait. That night the young men sat up very late talking with their father, and did not lie down to sleep until after midnight, when, as their father directed, they lay side by side with their heads to the east.

17. The elder brother arose early, stirred the embers and made a fire, and soon the younger awoke. As they sat by the fire warming themselves, the elder one said: "Younger brother, I had a dream in the night; I dreamt I killed a buck deer." And the younger replied: "Elder brother, I, too, had such a dream, but that which I killed was a doe." The old man heard their words and rose, saying, "It is well, my children; go out and try again." They went out to visit their traps. The first one they came to had fallen; they lifted the stone and found under it the body of a rat. So each one in turn, as they visited it was found to have fallen, killing in its fall some small animal; and they returned to the lodge with twelve little creatures for their food. Then the old man told them to take their bows and arrows and hunt for deer. "Hunt," said he, "to the east, the west, and the north, if you will, but do not pass to the south of the lodge." With these instructions they set out, each one in a different direction. The elder brother had not traveled far when he saw a herd of deer and shot one of the number. He skinned it, cut it up, took the backbone, hide, and tallow, and hung the rest in a tree. As he drew near the house, he saw his younger brother approaching from a different direction with the hide and meat of a doe. When they entered the hut, the old man asked which of the two deer was shot first. The elder brother answered: "I think mine was, for I killed it early this morning, soon after I left the house."

"Well," said the father, "this skin of the first slain is mine; go and stretch it and dry it for me with care." After this they went out hunting every day for twelve days, but fortune seemed to have deserted them; they killed no more game; and at the end of that time their supply of meat was exhausted. Then the old man said: "It always takes four trials before you succeed. Go out once more, and if you kill a deer do not dress it, but leave it as it is."

18. On the following day they left the lodge together and did not take separate trails. Soon they killed a deer, and the younger brother said: "What shall we now do with it, since our father has told us not to skin it and not to cut it up?" The elder brother said: "I know not. Return to the lodge and ask our father what we must do." Then the younger brother returned to his father and the latter instructed him thus: "Cut the skin around the neck; then carefully take the skin from the head, so as to remove the horns, ears, and all other parts, without tearing the skin anywhere. Leave such an amount of flesh with the nose and lips that they will not shrivel and lose their shape when they dry. Then take the skin from the body, which skin will again be mine. One of you must take out the pluck and carry that in the hide to me; the other will bring the skin of the head and the meat. Let him who bears the pluck come in advance, and stop not till he comes directly to me, and he must hand it to me and to no one else." The younger brother went back and told all this to the elder. They dressed the deer as they were bidden; the younger put the pluck in the skin and went in advance, and the elder followed with the venison and the skin of the head. When they reached the hogán, the father said: "Where is the atcai?" (pluck) and the younger said: "It is in the skin." "Take it out," said the old man, "and hang it on yonder mountain mahogany." The young man did as he was bidden. The father advanced with his bow and arrow and handed them to the elder brother, who placed the arrow on the string and held the bow. The old man put his hands on top of those of his son and together they drew the bow. The former took careful aim at the pluck and let the arrow fly. It struck the object and penetrated both heart and lungs so far that the point protruded on the opposite side. Then the old man told his son to seize the arrow by the point and draw it completely through, which was done. Next he made his son stand close to the pluck, looking towards it, and while his son was in this position he blew on him in the direction of the pluck. "Now," said the father, "whenever you want to kill a buck, even if there is neither track nor sign of deer in sight, you have only to shoot into the tse'isçázi (mountain mahogany, *Cercocarpus parvifolius*) and you will find a dead deer where your arrow strikes; while if you wish to kill a female deer you will shoot your arrow into the awètsal (cliff rose, *Cowania mexicana*) and you will find a doe there." When all this was done they prepared the skin of the head, under the old man's directions. To keep the skin of the neck open they put into it a wooden hoop.

They sewed up the mouth, left the eyeholes open, stuffed the skin with hay, and hung it in a tree to dry, where it would not get smoky or dusty. They cut places in the neck through which the hunter might see. The skin of the doe which the younger brother had killed some time before, and which had been tanned in the mean time, they painted red and gray, to make it look like the skin of an antelope. They prepared two short sticks, about the length of the forearm; these were to enable the hunter to move with ease and hold his head at the proper height when he crept in disguise on the deer. During the next four days no work was done, except that the elder brother practiced in imitating the walk of the deer.

19. From the camp where these things happened they moved to a place called Tse'-lakàï-iá' (White Standing Rock). Before they went to hunt or gather seeds, the old man desired that they should all help to build the hogán (hut); so all went to work together, men and women, and the hogán was completed, inside and outside, in four days.

20. The morning following the completion of the hogán, the father sent the young men out again, directing them, as before, not to go to the south. They went off together, and soon espied a herd of deer. The elder brother put on the deer mask and began to imitate the motions of the animal, asking his younger brother what he thought of the mimicry. When the latter gave his approval, the elder brother said, "Steal round to the other side of the herd and when they see you they will come in my direction." He waited, and when he saw that his brother had got to the other side of the herd, he selected a big fat buck as his special object, and began to move towards him, walking and pawing the ground like a deer, and rubbing his antlers against the trees. Soon the buck began to approach the hunter, but the latter kept his head constantly turned toward the deer the better to maintain his disguise. Presently the buck came quite close to the Indian, when the latter sped his arrow and brought the quarry down. They carried the meat home and the old man demanded that the meat and skin should all be his in payment for his advice. This was the third time he had advised them and the third time he had received a gift for his service. He directed that the meat should be cut into pieces and hung in the trees to dry, and that the skin should be stretched and dried for his bed.

21. Next day the elder brother desired the younger to stay at home, saying that he would like to hunt alone. As usual, the old man warned him against the south and directed him to hunt in the country north of the hogán. He set out, accordingly, to the north; but he returned at night without any game. Again on the following morning he set out alone, and this time went to the west, as his father had directed. He hunted all day without success, until near sunset, when it was time for him to return. Then he remembered what his father had told him of the shrubs that would always have deer for his arrow. Looking around he saw a cliff rose, into which he shot his dart, and at the same instant

he observed a deer falling in the shrub. He ran to the spot and found a dead doe. When he had skinned and dressed it, he could discover no high tree at hand that he might hang it on to keep it safe from the wolves, so he laid the meat on the top of the cliff rose, spread the skin over it, stuck an arrow upright on the top of it, and went home. On his way he often said to himself, "Why does my father bid me never to go to the south?" He pondered much on the subject, and before he reached the hut he had determined to satisfy his curiosity and to go to the south on the first good opportunity. When he got home he told where he had laid the meat, and, fearing that the crows or coyotes might get at it, he begged his brother to hasten and bring it in. When the meat came he asked that a piece might be broiled for his lunch on the hunt next day. All that night the thought of his father's prohibition continued to haunt his mind and would not be dismissed.

22. On the morrow, when he went forth on his hunt, his father gave him the usual injunctions, saying: "Hunt in any direction from the lodge that you will; but go not to the south." He departed as if he were going to the east; but when he got out of sight from the hogán he turned round to the south and pursued his way in that direction. He went on until he came to the San Juan River, and he forded it at a place a little above Beautiful Under the Cottonwoods, where they had crossed it before. He went on to a place called Tyèl-sakać (Erect Cat-Tail Rushes) and thence to a place called Dsiskíć (Clay Hill). Here he laid his deer skin mask and his weapons on the ground and climbed the hill to observe the surrounding country for game. But instead of looking south in the direction in which he was going he looked to the north, the country in which dwelt his people. Before him were the beautiful peaks of Ćepéntsa, with their forested slopes. The clouds hung over the mountain, the showers of rain fell down its sides, and all the country looked beautiful. And he said to the land, "Aqalàni!" (greeting), and a feeling of loneliness and homesickness came over him, and he wept and sang this song:

> That flowing water! That flowing water!
> My mind wanders across it.
> That broad water! That flowing water!
> My mind wanders across it.
> That old age water! That flowing water!
> My mind wanders across it.

23. The gods heard his song and they were about to gratify his wishes. He was destined to return to Ćepéntsa, but not in the manner he most desired. Had he gazed to the south when he ascended the hill, instead of to the north, it might have been otherwise.

24. He wiped away his tears and went down to the place where he had laid his mask and arms at the foot of the hill. He put on his buckskin coat and was just putting on his mask, but had not quite drawn it down over his head, when he heard a noise to the south and, looking

around, he saw a great crowd on horseback riding towards him. To
see better he drew off his mask, and then observed that they were
dividing into two lines as they advanced; a moment later he was surrounded. The horsemen were of the tribe of Ute, a people whose
language he did not understand. One young man rode up close to the
Navajo, aimed an arrow at the breast of the latter and drew it to the
head; but just as he was about to release it an old man began to address the party in a loud voice and the young warrior lowered his arrow and relaxed his bow. Then the speaker dismounted, approached
the captive, and seized him by the arm. For a long time there was
much loud talking and discussion among the Ute. Now one would
harangue the party and then another would make a speech, but after a
while the dispute ceased and the old man motioned to the Navajo to
move on. They made him trot while they followed him on horseback
in a semicircle, so that they could guard him and watch his movements.
Soon they came to Tyèl·saka¢; shortly afterward they crossed the San
Juan. That night they camped near Çepéntsa, where they watched
him closely all night and gave him nothing to eat. They bound his
feet firmly together, tied his hands behind his back, and threw an un-
tanned buckskin over him before they lay down to sleep.

25. They set out on their journey again early in the morning. At
Çòinçeski‘ (Scattered Springs) they stopped for a little while to eat, but
the only food they gave the Navajo was the full of his palm of service
berries. When they arrived on the south side of Çòtsosi (Narrow Water)
they halted for the night and a number went out to hunt. Among them
they secured two deer, one large and one small; the feet of these they
gave to their captive for his supper. Next morning they gave him a
piece of liver, half of which he ate and the rest he kept. They moved
on rapidly and rested for the night at Dsil·nahoyàl, where there was a
spring. They had given him nothing to eat all that day, and at night
they gave him nothing; so it was well for him that he had secreted part
of the liver. This he ate after dark. On the third morning he had to
set out fasting and had to go on foot as usual. About noon, however,
one of the Ute took pity on him and lent him a horse to ride, while
the owner of the horse walked all the afternoon. That night they arrived at the bank of a large river, and here they gave him to understand, by signs, that this was the last river they would cross until they
got home. Beyond the river there was nothing in sight but a great
plain.

26. By the light of the morning, however, on the next day, he dis-
cerned some mountains showing their points faintly above the northern
horizon. To these the Ute pointed and motioned to him to go ahead.
They did not follow him immediately; but saddled up at their leisure
while the Navajo went on. Though he was now for some time alone
on the trail and out of sight of his captors, he knew that he could
not escape; all around and before him was a desert plain where he could

not discover a single hiding place; so he trudged on, tired and hungry and sorrowing, and he wept all along the way. At noon they gave him another handful of berries.

27. At night they came to a plain situated between four mountains, one on the east, one on the south, one on the west, and one on the north, and here there was a great encampment of Ute, whose tents were scattered around in different places on the plain. There was one tent whose top was painted black and whose base was painted white and which had a forked pole set in the ground in front of it. To this his master, the old man who had saved his life and taken him by the arm on the occasion of his capture, led him, while the rest of the war party departed to their respective tents. The old man hung his own arms and accouterments on the pole, and the slave, following his example, hung his deer skin mask and robe on the forks and laid his crutches against the pole, and he prayed to the head of the deer, saying:

Whenever I have appealed to you, you have helped me, my pet.
Once you were alive. my pet.
Take care that I do not die, my pet.
Watch over me.

When he had finished his prayer an old man came and danced around him, and when the latter had done an old woman approached with a whistle in her hand and she whistled all around him. This was for joy because they had captured one of an alien tribe. Then his master motioned to him to go into the tent. Here he was given a large bowl of berries of which he ate his fill, and he was allowed to lie down and sleep undisturbed until morning.

28. Next morning the Ute began to enter the tent. They came one by one and in small groups until after a while there was a considerable crowd present. Then they gave the Navajo to understand by signs that they wished to know for what purpose he wore the mask and the buckskin. He answered that he used them for no particular purpose, but only for a whim. They repeated the question three times very pointedly and searchingly, but he continued to make evasive replies. The fourth time they addressed him they charged him to tell the truth and speak quickly, reminding him that he was a prisoner whose life was in the hands of his captors and telling him that if he did not disclose the use of his mask and robe he would be killed before sunset, while if he revealed the secret his life would be spared. He pondered but a short time over their words and determined to tell them the truth. So he explained to them the use of the mask and the robe in deceiving the deer and told the wonderful power he had of getting game by shooting into certain bushes. At dark they sent in two young men to be initiated into his mysteries. He began by giving them a full account of all his father had done and all he had shown him; he then taught them how to build the sweat-house, how to make the mask, how to shoot the pluck, and how to walk like a deer, and he made them prac-

tice the walk and the motions of the animal. All this occupied eleven days.

29. On the twelfth day the Ute went out to hunt, leaving few men in camp. There was a small inclosure of brushwood close to the tent; in it were two high poles on which skins were dressed. His master left him, that day, two skins to prepare, and he set to work at them and labored hard scraping and rubbing them until about noon, when he felt hungry and went into the tent to see if he could find anything to eat. He opened a bag and found it to contain dried meat; he put some of this on the coals and sat down to wait till it was done. As he watched the meat cooking he heard a noise at the deer skin door of the tent and, looking up, he beheld an old woman crawling in on her hands and knees. She passed once around the fire and went out at the door again, but before she disappeared she turned her head and addressed him, saying: "My grandchild, do something for yourself." He paused a moment in wonder at the strange vision he had seen and the strange words he had heard, and then he rushed out of the tent to follow his visitor and see who she might be. He went around the tent four times; he gazed in every direction ; but no one was to be seen. During the rest of the day he worked but little. Occasionally he took up a stone and rubbed the hides; but most of the time he walked and loitered around, busy with his thoughts.

30. After sunrise the hunters returned with an abundance of meat. They came to the great lodge where the master of the Navajo dwelt; they extended its circumference by removing the pegs at the bottom; they stored the goods of the owner away at the outer edge, so as to leave a clear space in the center, and made everything ready for the reception of a large number of guests. After dark a great number gathered in the tent and the captive was ordered by his master to bring some water. He took two wicker bottles to a neighboring spring, filled them, and laid them on the ground beside the spring, while he went to gather some plants to stick into the mouths of the bottles as stopples. As he went he heard a voice saying "Hist!" and looking in the direction whence it came he saw a form sitting in the water ; it wore a mask like the head of a great owl and it was smoking a pipe. When he turned towards it, it said, "You walk around like one without sense or knowledge. Why don't you do something for yourself? When next you hear my voice it will be well for you if you walk towards it."

31. The voice ceased and the form of the owl-man vanished. Then the Navajo put the stopples into the vessels and carried them back. When he returned he observed that two large dogs were tied to the door, one on each side, and that three doors had been added to the lodge during his absence, so that now there were four doors covering the doorway. When he entered he found the lodge filled with Ute and he saw four bags of tobacco and four pipes lying near the fire, one at each cardinal point of the compass. He observed a very old man and a very

old woman seated at the door, one on each side. A cord tied to the old woman passed round the edge of the lodge on one side, behind the spectators, to the west, and another cord, tied to the man, passed round on the opposite side of the lodge. His master bade him sit down in the west, and when he was seated one of the cords was tied to his wrists and one to his ankles, and thus he was secured to the old pair.

32. Now he feared more than ever for his safety; he felt sure that his captors contemplated his death by torture. The pipes were lit and the council began. The talking in the strange tongue that he could not understand had lasted long into the night, when he fancied that he heard the voice of the Yèbit-cai (Anglicized, Yày-bi-chy or Gay-bi chy) above the din of human voices, saying "hu'hu'hu'hu" in the far distance. He strained his attention and listened well, and after a while he felt certain that he heard the voice again nearer and louder. It was not long until the cry was repeated for the third time, and soon after the captive heard it once more, loudly and distinctly, immediately to the west of the lodge. Then there was a sound as of footsteps at the door, and the white lightning entered through the smoke-hole and circled around the lodge, hanging over the heads of the council. But the Ute heard not the voice which the Navajo heard and saw not the vision he beheld. Soon the Yàybichy (Qastcèëlçi) entered the lodge and standing on the white lightning, said: "What is the matter with you, my grandchild? You take no thought about anything. Something you must do for yourself, or else, in the morning you will be whipped to death — that is what the council has decided. Pull

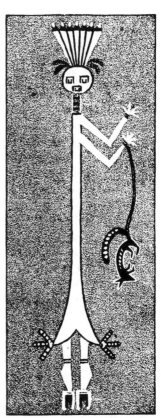

FIG. 50. Qastcèëlçi, from a dry painting of the klèdji-qaçàl.

out four pegs from the bottom of the tent, push it open there, and then you can shove things through." The Navajo answered, "How shall I do it? See the way I am tied! I am poor! See how I am wound up!" But Qastcèëlçi again said: "When you leave, take with you those bags filled with embroideries and take with you tobacco from the pouches near the fire." Scarcely had Qastcèëlçi disappeared when the Navajo heard a voice overhead, and a bird named qocçò¢i flew down through the smoke-hole, hovered four times around the lodge over the heads of the Ute, and departed by the way it had entered. In a moment after it had disappeared a few of the Ute began to nod and close their eyes; soon the others showed signs of drowsiness; some stretched themselves out on the ground overpowered with sleep; others rose and departed from time to time, singly and in little groups, to seek their lodges and repose there. The last to drop asleep were the old man and the old woman who sat at the door; but at length their chins fell upon their bosoms. Then the Navajo, fearing no watchers, went to work and loosened the cords that bound him; he lifted, from the inside, some of the pegs which held the edge of the tent, and shoved out the two bags of embroideries which Qastcèëlçi had told him to take. Passing out through the door of the lodge, where he found both the watch-dogs sound asleep, and taking with him the cords with which he had been tied and some of the tobacco, he went round to the back of the lodge, where he had put the bags; these he tied with the cords in such a manner that they would make an easily balanced double bundle. He shouldered his bundle and was all ready to start.

33. At this moment he heard, at a little distance to the south of where he stood, the hoot of an owl. Instantly recollecting the words of the owl-like form which he had encountered at the spring at night-fall, he set off in the direction from which the call proceeded. He had not walked far until he came to a precipitous bluff formed by two branch-ing cañons, and it seemed at first impossible for him to proceed farther. Soon, however, he noticed a tall spruce tree, which grew beside the precipice from the foot to the summit, for the day had now begun to dawn and he could see objects more clearly. At this juncture Qastcèëlçi again appeared to him and said: "How is it, my grandchild, that you are still here? Get on the top of that spruce tree and go down into the cañon on it." The Navajo stretched out his hand to seize the top of the tree, but it swayed away from his grasp. "See, my grandfather," he said to Qastcèëlçi, "it moves away from me; I cannot reach it." Then Qastcèëlçi flung the white lightning around the top of the tree, as an Indian flings his lasso around the neck of a horse, and drew it in to the edge of the cliff. "Descend," he commanded the Indian, "and when you reach the bottom take four sprays from the tree, each from a different part. You may need them in the future." So the Navajo went down, took the four sprays as he was bidden and put them under his robe.

34. At the base of the bluff he again met Qastcèëlçi, and at this moment he heard a noise, as of a great and distant tumult, which seemed to come from above and from beyond the edge of the cliff whence they had descended. From moment to moment it grew louder and came nearer, and soon the sounds of angry voices could be distinguished. The Ute had discovered the flight of their captive and were in hot pur-suit. "Your enemies are coming for you," said the divine one; "but yonder small holes on the opposite side of the cañon are the doors of my dwelling, where you may hide. The bottom of the cañon is strewn

with large rocks and fallen trees ; it would take you much time and hard labor to get over these if I did not help you; but I will do something to make your way easy." As he said this he blew a strong breath, and instantly a great white rainbow spanned the cañon. The Navajo tried to step on this in order to cross, but it was so soft that his feet went through ; he could not step on it. Qastcèëlçi stood beside him and laughed at his fruitless attempts to get on the rainbow. After he had enjoyed this sport sufficiently the ye (Anglicized, gay or yay) blew another strong breath, when at once the rainbow became as hard as ice and they both crossed it with ease. When they reached the opposite wall of the cañon Qastcèëlçi pointed to a very small hole in the cliff and said, "This is the door of my lodge; enter!" By this time the shouts of the Ute sounded very loud in the ears of the terrified fugitive and it seemed to him that his pursuers must have reached the edge of the opposite cliff, where they would not be long before they would see him ; still, hard as he tried to enter the cave, he could not succeed ; the hole was not big enough for him to put his head in. The Yàybichy roared with laughter and slapped his hands together as he witnessed the abject fear and the fruitless efforts of the Navajo. When he had laughed enough he blew on the little hole and it spread instantly into a large orifice, through which they both entered with ease. They passed through three rooms and stopped in the fourth. Here Qastcèëlçi took the bags from the back of the Navajo, opened them, and drew from them some beautifully garnished clothing—a pair of moccasins, a pair of long-fringed leggings, and a shirt. He arrayed himself in these and went out, leaving the Navajo in the cave. As soon as his rescuer was gone the fugitive heard loud noises without and the sound of many angry voices, which continued for a long, long time. At last they died away and were heard no more. The Ute had tracked him to the edge of the cliff where he got on the tree ; but there they lost his trail and searched all the neighborhood to see if they could regain it; hence the noises. When all was silent Qastcèëlçi returned and said, "Your enemies have departed; you can leave in safety." So, taking a tanned elk skin to cover his back and a pair of new moccasins to protect his feet, the Navajo set out from the cave.

35. It was nightfall when he emerged. He turned his face in the direction of his home and walked rapidly all the night. As day dawned he began to feel hopeful ; but, ere the sun rose, distant sounds, which grew louder and louder, reached his ear. He knew them to be the voices of his pursuers and again he became sorely afraid. He hurried on and came near the foot of a high isolated pinnacle of rock, whose top appeared to be inaccessible. Glancing to the summit, however, he beheld standing there a black mountain sheep. Thinking that this singular vision was sent to him as a sign from the yays (gods) and boded well for him, he came to the base of the rock, when the sheep addressed him, saying: "My grandson, come around to the other side of the rock and you will

find a place where you may ascend." He went around as he was bidden and saw the cleft in the rock, but it was too narrow for him to climb in it. Then the sheep blew into the cleft and it spread out so wide that he entered it easily and clambered to the summit. Here he found the sheep standing in four tracks, marked or sunken in the rock, one hoof in each track, and under the center of his body was a small hole in the rock. Into this hole the sheep bade him enter; but he replied that the hole was too small. Then the sheep blew on the hole and it spread so wide open that both the man and the sheep entered easily and descended into the heart of the rock. Here there were again four apartments; two of them were blue and two were black; rainbows extended in all directions through them. In the fourth room, which was black, the sheep left the Navajo to rest, and departed. Soon the fugitive heard, as on the previous day, when he lay hidden in the cave of Qastcèëlçi, the voices of the angry Ute calling and haranguing all around the rock, and he continued to hear them for a very long time. Soon after the clamor ceased the sheep returned to him to notify him that his enemies had withdrawn and that he could set out on his journey again without fear.

36. He journeyed homeward all the night, and when daylight began to appear he found himself on the banks of the stream where the Ute slept the night before they reached their tents, when they bore him home a captive. Here again he heard in the distance the voices of his pursuers and he hastened his steps. Presently he met a little old man sitting on the ground and cleaning cactus fruit. The old man had a sharp nose, little bright eyes, and a small moustache growing on each side of his upper lip. At once the Navajo recognized him as the Bush-rat (*Neotoma mexicana*). The latter asked the traveler where he came from. "Oh, I am just roaming around here," was the answer. But the rat, not satisfied, repeated his question three times, in a manner which gave the Navajo to understand that his answer was not credited. So at last he answered truthfully that he was a Navajo who had been captured by the Ute, and that he was fleeing homeward from his captors, who were at that moment close behind him in pursuit. "It is well," said the rat, "that you have told me this, for I think I can save you. On yonder hillside there is a flat rock, and round about it are piled many little sticks and stones. It is my home, and I will guide you thither." He led the Indian to the rock and, showing him a small hole under it, bade him stoop low and place his head near the hole. As the Navajo obeyed the rat blew a strong breath on the hole, which at once opened wide enough to let the visitor in. The rat followed immediately behind him as he entered. Inside of the den there were an old woman, two young men, and two young women. These constituted the family of the Bush-rat, who left the den as soon as the stranger was safely housed. Soon the voices of the pursuing Ute were again heard around the rock and at the mouth of the den, and the Navajo sat a long time

in silence listening to them. After a while the rat woman said to him, "You seem to be tired and hungry. Will you have something to eat?" and he answered, "Yes; I am very hungry and would like some food." On hearing this she went into one corner of her dwelling, where were many chips and bones and shells of seeds and skins of fruits, and she brought him some of these and offered them to him; but at this moment the wind god whispered into his ear and warned him not to partake of the refuse; so he said to the woman, "My mother, I can not eat these things." Then she went to another corner of the den, where there was another pile of débris; but again the wind god prompted him and again he refused. After this she visited in turn two other piles of trash in the corners of her lodge and tried to make him accept it as food, but he still rejected it. Now, while he had been sitting in the lodge he had not failed to look around him, and he had observed a long row of wicker jars standing at one side. At one end of the row was a black vessel and at the other end a white vessel. When she at length asked him, "What food is it that you would have, my son?" the wind god whispered to him, "Ask her for that which is in the jars at the end of the row," and he replied, "I will take some food from the black jar and some from the white jar." She removed the stopples from the jars. From the black vessel she took nuts of the piñon and fruit of the yucca and from the white vessel she took cherries and cactus fruit, all of which he received in the folded corner of his elk robe. He was just about to partake of some of the nice fruit when again he heard the low voice of the wind god. This time it said, "Eat not the food of the rats in the home of the rats, if you would not become a rat; wait till you go out to night." Much as he longed for the food, after hearing this, he tasted it not, but held it in the fold of the elk skin. Late in the day they were all astonished by hearing a loud rattling noise at the mouth of the cave, and, looking in that direction, saw the end of a big stick, which was thrust viciously from time to time into the opening and poked around in different directions; but it was not long enough to reach to the place where they sat. "What is that?" said the woman. "Oh," answered the Navajo, "that is the Ute, who have trailed me to this hole and hope to kill me by poking that stick in here." The old rat watched from a secret place outside all the actions of the Ute, and when he came home at night he asked his family if the stick had hurt any of them. "We saw only the end of it," they replied. He then turned to the Navajo and said, "Your pursuers have disappeared; you may go out without fear."

37. He trudged wearily on all night, and at dawn he was beside the high volcanic rocks at Çòtsosi, another place where his captors had halted with him. There is one place where the rocky wall is quite smooth. As he was passing this place he heard a voice saying, "Sh!" He looked all around him, but saw nothing that could have made the sound. He was about to pass on when he again heard the voice, and,

looking around, he again saw no one. The fourth time that this happened, however, he observed in the smooth part of the rock a door standing open and a little animal called Kleyatcini looking out at him. As he stood gazing at the sharp nose and the bright eyes the distant voices of his pursuers sounded again in his ears and the little animal bade him enter and hide himself. As the Navajo entered the Kleyatcini passed out and closed the door behind him. The fugitive was not long in his place of concealment when the clamor made by the foiled pursuers was again heard, but it ceased sooner than usual. It was not yet sunset when the little animal returned to announce that the Ute had gone from the neighborhood. When the Navajo stepped out of the hole in the rock, Kleyatcini pointed out to him the mountains in which his home lay and counseled him to travel directly towards them.

38. He pursued his way in the direction indicated to him all night, and at break of day he found himself walking between a pair of low hills of clay which stood close together, and once more he heard behind him the voices of his enemies and the trampling of their horses. But now his good friend Qastcĕëlçi appeared to him and said to him: "My grandchild, are you still here? Have you come only thus far?" "I am here," cried the Navajo, "and oh, my grandfather, I could do no better. Look at my limbs! See how sore and swollen they are! I am exhausted and feel that I cannot flee much farther before my enemies." "Go, then," said Qastcĕëlçi, "to that hill which is the farther from us and climb to the top of it; but, when you are taking the very last step which will place you on the summit, shut your eyes as you make that step." The Navajo hastened to the hill, and, weary as he was, he soon ascended it. As he lifted his foot to take the last step he closed his eyes, as the yay had bidden him. When he felt his foot again on the earth he opened his eyes, and lo! instead of having a little hill under his feet, he stood on the summit of a great mountain peak, seamed with deep cañons, bordered with rugged rocks, and clothed with great forests of pine and spruce; while far away on the plain at the foot of the mountain — so far that he could scarcely discern them — were his baffled pursuers, and beside him stood Qastcĕëlçi. The latter pointed out to him many familiar places in the distance — the valley of the San Juan and Dsilyi‘-qojòni (Beautiful in the Mountains), where he and his people first lived. He rested securely on the mountain top all day.

39. At sunset he went on his way again. When daylight began to appear he crossed the San Juan. Soon after, while journeying on over an open plain, he once more heard the Ute on his trail. He now felt very sad and hopeless, for his limbs were so stiff and swollen that every motion gave him pain and he could hardly drag himself along. But at this moment he became conscious that he was not alone, and glancing to one side he saw Niltci, the wind god, walking with him. And Niltci brought a great dark whirlwind, which roared a moment beside them and then buried its point in the ground and dug a deep hole

there; it dug a cavern with four chambers. Then dark clouds gathered and rain began to fall. "Have you anything with you that may help you?" asked the god. "I have nothing," said the Navajo, "but four sprays of spruce, which the Yàybichy bade me pluck from the tree on which I descended into the cañon the night I left the Ute camp." "They will do," said the wind god. "Make quickly four balls of mud and thrust through each ball a twig of the spruce, and lay them on the ground so that the tops of the twigs will point towards your enemies." The Navajo did as he was commanded. Then Niltci blew the twigs and mud balls in the direction of the pursuers and told the Navajo to descend into the retreat which the whirlwind had formed. He went down and rested secure, while he heard overhead great peals of thunder, the loud rushing of the tempest, and the heavy pattering of enormous hailstones, to bring which the mud balls had been made. The noises of the storm died away, and about midday Niltci came into the cave and said to the man: "Come forth; your enemies have been dispersed. Many have been killed by the hail, and the rest have gone towards their homes." Then the Navajo came up out of the ground and set out in the direction of his old home at Dsilyi'-qojòni.

40. It was about sunset when he reached the top of the mountain. The snow began to fall heavily and a strong wind began to blow. He walked on to the western brow of the mountain, where there was a great precipice. Here the storm blew with such violence that he could scarcely stand, and yet the precipice was so steep that he did not see how he could get down. But soon, as on a former occasion of this kind, he discovered a spruce tree which grew against the side of the precipice, and at the same time Qastcèëlçi appeared to him again and directed him to go down on the spruce tree. He did so, and when he reached the bottom he found the yay there awaiting him. He addressed Qastcèëlçi: "Oh, my grandfather, I am tired and sore and sleepy. I would like to lie down under this tree and sleep." But the god answered, "Go, my grandchild, to yonder fire and rest," and he pointed to a distant gleam on the side of a mountain which lay beyond a very deep valley. "No, my grandfather," cried the Navajo, "I am weary and my limbs are sore and weak; I can not travel so far." "I will help you," said the yay, and as he spoke he spanned the valley with a flash of lightning, over which he led the man to the distant mountain. They reached it at a point close to the fire; but the moment they stood again on the firm earth Qastcèëlçi and the fire vanished. The man was bewildered and at a loss what to do. He walked around the mountain a short distance and then changed his mind and walked back to the place from which he started. Here he found Qastcèëlçi awaiting him. The yay spoke not a word, but pointed down into the valley and led the way thither. At the bottom of the valley they came to a great hole in the ground; the yay pointed in and again led the way. As they advanced into the cave the air grew warmer. In a little while they discovered a bright

fire on which there was no wood. Four pebbles lay on the ground together: a black pebble in the east, a blue one in the south, a yellow
one in the west, and a white one in the north; from these the flames
issued forth. Around the fire lay four bears, colored and placed to cor-
respond with the pebbles. When the strangers approached the fire
the bears asked them for tobacco, and when the former replied that
they had none the bears became angry and thrice more demanded it.
When the Navajo fled from the Ute camp he had helped himself from
one of the four bags which the council was using and had taken a
pipe, and these he had tied up in his skin robe; so when the fourth
demand was made he filled the pipe and lighted it at the fire. He
handed the pipe to the black bear, who, taking but one whiff, passed it
to the blue bear and immediately fell senseless. The blue bear took
two whiffs and passed the pipe, when he too fell over in a state of un-
consciousness. The yellow bear succumbed after the third whiff, and
the white bear, in the north, after the fourth whiff. Now the Navajo
knocked the ashes and tobacco out of his pipe and rubbed the latter on
the feet, legs, abdomen, chest, shoulders, forehead, and mouth of each
of the bears in turn, and they were at once resuscitated. He replaced
the pipe in the corner of his robe. When the bears recovered they
assigned to the Navajo a place on the east side of the fire where he
might lie all night, and they brought out their stores of corn meal and
tciltcin and other berries and offered them to him to eat; but Qastcèëlçi
warned him not to touch the food and again disappeared. So, hungry
as he was, the Indian lay down supperless to sleep. When he woke
in the morning the bears again offered food, which he again declined,
saying he was not hungry. Then they showed him how to make the
bear kethàwns, or sticks to be sacrificed to the bear gods, and they
drew from one corner of the cave a great sheet of cloud, which they
unrolled, and on it were painted the forms of the yays of the cultivated
plants. As he departed the bears said, "There are others in these
parts who have secrets to tell you. Yonder is Tsenástci, where many
dwell." So he set forth for Tsenástci (Circle of Red Stones.)

41. As he passed down the valley he heard a loud rushing noise be
hind him, and looking around he beheld a tornado. The air was filled
with logs and uprooted trees, borne along by the great storm. It came
nearer and seemed to be advancing to destroy him. He was terrified
and cried out to the storm: "Ciyèïcçe, Dsilyi' Neyáni. Qaïlàçi?" ("'Tis
I, Reared Within the Mountains. Who art thou?") The tempest recognized him and subsided, and in its place appeared four men in the shape
of the glòï or weasel. The four weasel men showed him how to make
the glòï-bikeçan, or sacrificial sticks of the glòï. What name the Navajo bore before this time the ancient tale does not tell us; but from
the moment he said these words he was called among the gods Dsilyi'
Neyáni, and was afterwards known by this name among his people.

42. After this adventure he continued on his way to Tsenástci. He had not journeyed far when he met the wind god, who said to him: "Those whom you will meet at Tsenástci are evil ones; therefore I will be with you and will walk before you." When they came to Tsenástci they found a hole in the rocks guarded by two great rattlesnakes, one on each side, and covered by two piñon trees, for a door. When the travelers drew near, the serpents showed signs of great anger, and when the former approached the door the reptiles shook their rattles violently, thrust out their tongues, and struck at the intruders as though they would bite them; but they did not bite. Niltci thrust aside the piñon trees; he and his companions entered, and, when they had passed within, the piñon trees, moving of their own accord, closed the entrance behind them. Within they encountered a bald headed old man who had only a little tuft of hair over each ear. This was Klictsò, the Great Serpent. He asked Niltci who his human companion was, and the wind god answered that he was a Navajo who had been captured by the Ute, but had escaped from them and had suffered many hardships. On hearing this Klictsò showed the Indian how to make the kethàwns, now known to the Navajo shamans as klictsò-bikeçan, or sacrificial sticks of the Great Serpent, and he told him how to plant these sacrifices.

43. From the home of Klictsò they went to a place called Tse'binàyol (Wind Circles Around a Rock). When they drew near the place they heard loud peals of thunder and the lightning struck close to them in four different places. They were now approaching the home of the lightning gods; this is why destruction by the thunderbolt seemed to threaten them. Then the Navajo spoke to the lightning, as he had formerly spoken to the whirlwind, saying, "'Tis I, Reared Within the Mountains. Who art thou?" whereat the thunder and the lightning ceased, and the travelers walked on until they entered a house of black clouds, inside of a mountain, which was the house of I'çnì', the Lightning. He was bald, like the Great Serpent, having only a little tuft of hair over each ear. At each of the four sides of the room where I'çnì' sat was a lightning bird; that in the east was black, that in the south was blue, that in the west, yellow, and that in the north, white. From time to time the birds flashed lightning from their claws to the center of the room where the god sat, and the lightning was of the same color as the bird that emitted it. When the travelers entered I'çnì' said to Niltci, "Who is this that you have brought with you?" The latter answered, "It is a Navajo who has been a captive with the Ute and has escaped. He has suffered much. See how his knees and ankles are swollen." Then the Lightning showed him two kethàwns, such as the shamans now sacrifice under the name of i'çnì'-bikeçan, or sacrificial sticks of the lightning, and, having instructed him how to make and to plant these, he bade his visitors depart.

44. The next place they reached on their journey was Sàï byitsòzi (Narrow Sand Hills). They entered the hill and came to the house of Kaȼlùgi, the Butterfly, a dwelling filled with butterflies and rainbows. They found Kaȼlùgi and his wife sitting there, and also Atsòsbebagàni (House of Feathers), who wore black leggins. Here Niltci disappeared and the woman had to put her questions to the Navajo. She inquired, as the others had done, who he was, and he briefly told her his story. She arose, went out, and presently returned with a large basin made of a beautiful white shell; this was filled with water and soap root. She laid it before the Navajo, saying, "You are about to visit some fair and beautiful people, and it is proper that you should bathe your body and wash your hair well." When he had finished his bath he of the house of feathers took fine corn meal and applied it to the feet, the knees, the abdomen, and the other parts of the body which are usually touched in healing ceremonies. Then, under the directions of Atsòs-bebagàni, the Navajo rubbed his whole body with meal to dry himself and painted his face white with glee (white earth). House of Feathers next brought in small bundles of the following plants: tcilȼelgísi (*Gutierrezia euthamiæ*), çoikal (*Artemesia trifida*), .tséji, and tlo'nasçási (*Bouteloua hirsuta*), burned them to charcoal, and directed the Indian to blacken his legs and forearms with this substance. When this was done he put spots of white on the black, and, in short, painted him as the akáninili, or courier (Fig. 52) se nt out to summon guests to the dance, is painted to this day in the ceremonies of the dsilyídje qaçàl. When the painting was done Kaȼlùgi Esçàya (Butterfly Woman) took hold of his hair and pulled it downward and stretched it until it grew in profusion down to his ankles. Then she pressed and worked his body and face all over until she molded him into a youth of the most beautiful form and feature. They gave him fine white moccasins and a collar of beaver skin with a whistle attached to it; they put the kàbasçau, or plumed sticks to represent wings, on his arms, and altogether dressed and adorned him as the akáninili is dressed and adorned. The woman gave him white corn meal mixed with water to eat, and he slept all night in the house of the butterflies. In the morning the woman (or goddess, as we might better call her) laid two streaks of white lightning on the ground and bade him stand on them with one foot on each streak. "Now," she said, "the white lightning is yours; use it how and when you will." Then she told him to go to the top of the hill in which their house lay. When he ascended he found another house on the top, and in it he again met Kaȼlùgi and his wife, who awaited him there. He observed a streak of white lightning that spanned a broad valley, stretching from the hill on which he stood to a distant wooded mountain. "There," said Kaȼlùgi Esçàya, pointing to the lightning, "is the trail you must follow. It leads to yonder mountain, which is named Bistcàgi."

45. He followed the lightning trail and soon arrived at the house of Estsàn-ɉigìni (Holy Woman). The house was inside of a black mountain; but the lightning ended not until it went quite into the dwelling; so he had only to follow it to find his way in. The door was of trees. Within, on the east wall hung the sun and on the west wall hung the moon. Here he was shown the kethàwn which is called Estsàn-ɉigìni-bikeçàn, or the sacrificial stick of the holy woman, and was told how to make it and how to bury it. As he was about to depart from this place two of the wind gods and the butterfly god appeared to him, and the whole party of four set out for Tcùckai (Chusca Knoll of our geographers).

46. At this place they entered a house which was inside of the mountain. It was two stories high; it had four rooms on the first story and four on the second. It had four doorways, which were covered with trees for doors; in the east was a black spruce tree, in the south a blue spruce tree, in the west a yellow spruce tree, and in the north a white shining spruce tree. Here dwelt four of the Tcikè-cac-nátlehi (Maiden that Becomes a Bear). Their faces were white; their legs and forearms were covered with shaggy hair; their hands were like those of human beings; but their teeth were long and pointed. The first Tcikè-cac-nátlehi, it is said, had twelve brothers. She learned the art of converting herself into a bear from the coyote. She was a great warrior and invulnerable. When she went to war she took out and hid her vital organs, so that no one could kill her; when the battle was over she put them back in their places again. The maidens showed him how to make four kethàwns and told him how to bury them in order to properly sacrifice them.

47. From Tcùckai they went to Ninà-qoɉezgòç (Valley Surrounded on All Sides by Hills), near ₵epéntsa, where they found the house of the Tsilkè-ɉigìni (Holy Young Men), of whom there were four. There were, in the dwelling, four rooms, which had not smooth walls, but looked like rooms in a cavern; yet the house was made of water. A number of plumed arrows (kátso-yisçàn) were hanging on the walls, and each young man (standing one in the east, one in the south, one in the west, and one in the north) held such an arrow in his extended right hand. No kethàwn was given him; but he was bidden to observe well how the holy young warriors stood, that he might imitate them in the rites he should establish amongst men.

48. The next place they visited was Tse'ça-iskági (Rock that Bends Back), where they entered a house, striped within horizontally of many colors, and found eight more of the Tsilkè-ɉigìni (Holy Young Men). Two stood at each cardinal point and each one grasped a sapling which he held over his upturned mouth, as if about to swallow it. One of the young men addressed him, saying " Do thus. There are eight of us here; but when you do this in the dance that you will teach your people you need not have eight young men—six will be enough."

49. From here they went to Tcétcel-hyitsò (Big Oaks), to visit the home of Ϙigin-yosíni (yosíni is a species of squirrel). It was built of black water-slime (çraçlíç) and the door was of red sunbeams. On the east wall hung a big black log; on the south wall, a blue log; on the west wall, a yellow log; and on the north wall, a white log; in which logs the squirrels dwelt. Although they were squirrels, they were young men and young women, and looked very much like one another. All had red and black stripes on their backs. These taught him how to make and bury the kethàwns sacred to themselves.

50. Dsilninèla' (Last Mountain) is a conical, sharp pointed eminence, shaped like a Navajo hogán or lodge. It is black and has white streaks running down its sides. This was the next place they visited. Within the mountain was a house, whose door was of darkness and was guarded by Tcápani (the Bat) and an animal called Çautsò (of crepuscular or nocturnal habits). Here dwelt many young men and young women who were skunks (golíji), and they taught the Navajo wanderer how to make and how to bury the kethàwns which are sacred to the skunk.

51. The next place to which they went was Dsil-nikí¢i-àgi (Mountain Comes Down Steep), and here they found the place where Glo'dsilkàï (Abert's squirrel, *Sciurus aberti*) and Glo'dsiljíni dwelt. When the four entered, the squirrels said to them: "What do you want here? You are always visiting where you are not welcome." The gods replied: "Be not angry with us. This is a Navajo who was a captive among the Ute, but he has escaped and has suffered much. I'¢nì' (the Lightning) has bidden us to take him to the homes of all the ¢igìni (holy ones, supernatural beings); therefore we have brought him here." "It is well," said the squirrels; "but he is hungry and must have some food." They brought him piñon nuts, pine nuts, spruce nuts, and service berries; but the gods told him not to partake of the nuts or he would be changed into a squirrel, to eat only of the service berries. When he had finished his meal, the squirrels showed him how to make two kethàwns and how to bury them.

52. Now Niltci whispered: "Let us go to Dsilyà-içíu" (Four Doorways Under a Mountain), where dwells Ϙasàni (the Porcupine). His house was in a black mountain. At the eastern doorway there was a black spruce tree for a door. On the other sides there were no doors; the entrances were open. They found here four porcupine gods, two male and two female. They were colored according to the four cardinal hues. The black one stood in the east, the blue one in the south, the yellow one in the west, and the white one in the north. They instructed him concerning the kethàwns of the porcupines, and they offered him food, which consisted of the inner bark of different kinds of trees. But again, prompted by Niltci, he refused the food, saying that he was not able to eat food of that kind. "It is well," said the porcupines, "and now you may leave us."

53. "Off in this direction," whispered Niltci, pointing to the northeast, "is a place called Qoɟestsò (Where Yellow Streak Runs Down). Let us go thither." Here they entered a house of one room, made of black water. The door was of wind. It was the home of Tcal-ninéz (Long Frog), of Çoklíc (Water Snake), of Klickà (Arrow Snake), and of other serpents and animals of the water. It was called Abyèqoɟeçi' (They Came Together), because here the prophet of the dsilyídje qaçàl visited the home of the snakes and learned something of their mysteries. The ceremonies sacred to these animals belong to another dance, that of the qojòni-qaçàl (chant of terrestrial beauty); but in the mysteries learned in Abyèqoɟeçi' the two ceremonies are one. Here he was instructed how to make and to sacrifice four kethàwns. To symbolize this visit of Dsilyi' Neyáni and this union of the two ceremonies, the first sand picture is made. (See Plate XV.)

54. The next place they visited was Açànkikè, where there was a house built of the white rock crystal, with a door made of all sorts of plants. It was called Tsegàɟiniçini-behogan (House of Rock Crystal) and was the home of Tcikè-ɟigìni (Supernatural Young Woman, or Young Woman Goddess), who was the richest of all the ɟigìni. In the middle of the floor stood a large crystal in the shape of a kethàwn. Just as they were entering, Qastcëëlçi, who had disappeared from the Navajo's sight at the house of the bears, here rejoined him, and the party now numbered five. The apartment, when they came into it, was very small, but Qastcëëlçi blew on the walls, which extended thereat until the room was one of great size. The goddess showed the Navajo how to make two kethàwns and directed him how to dispose of them.

55. Thence they journeyed to Tsitsè-intyèli (Broad Cherry Trees), where, in a house of cherries with a door of lightning, there lived four gods named Dsilyi' Neyáni (Reared Within the Mountains). The Navajo was surprised to find that not only had they the same name as he had, but that they looked just like him and had clothes exactly the same as his. His companions said to him: "These are the gods in whose beautiful form the Butterfly goddess has molded you. These are the gods whose name you bear." The hosts bade their visitors be seated, and they ranged themselves around the fire, one at each of the cardinal points. Each held an arrow made of the cliff rose (*Cowania mexicana*) in his extended right hand. The head of the arrow was of stone, the fletching of eagle feathers, and the "breath feather" of the downy plume of the Tsenáhale (the Harpy of Navajo mythology). As they held the arrows they ejaculated, "ai', ai', ai', ai'," as they who dance the kátso-yisçàn do in the ceremonies to this day, and after the fourth ai' each one swallowed his arrow, head foremost, until the fletching touched his lips. Then he withdrew the arrow and they said: "Thus do we wish the Navajo to do in the dance which you will teach them; but they must take good care not to break off the arrowheads when they swallow and withdraw them." Such is the origin of the dance of the kátso-yisçàn, or

great plumed arrow. As they bade him good bye, one of them said to the Navajo: "We look for you," i. e., "We expect you to return to us," an intimation to him that when he left the earth he should return to the gods, to dwell among them forever.

56. From this place they journeyed on until they reached Açàdsil (Leaf Mountain), and found the house that was made of dew-drops (Çaçò-behogan) and that had a door made of plants of many different kinds. This was the home of the Bitsès-ninéz (Long Bodies), who were goddesses. When they rose, as the strangers entered, the plumes on their heads seemed to touch the heavens, they were so very tall. The goddesses said to Dsilyi' Neyáni, "We give you no kethàwn, but look at us well and remember how we appear, for in your ceremonies you must draw our picture; yet draw us not, as we now stand, in the east, the south, the west, and the north; but draw us as if we all stood in the east." This is the origin of the second picture that is painted on the sand. (Plate XVI.)

57. Leaving the House of Dew they proceeded to Çonakàï (White Water Running Across). This was a stream which ran down the side of a hill and had its source in a great spring. Immediately above this spring was the home of Qastcèëlçi. The latter, as they approached his home, stopped at the foot of the hill and four times ordered his companions to go in advance; but four times they refused. After the last refusal Qastcèëlçi clapped his hands, uttered his cry of "hu' hu'hu' hu'!" and led the way. The house was of corn pollen; the door was of day light; the ceiling was supported by four white spruce trees; rainbows ran in every direction and made the house shine within with their bright and beautiful colors. Neither kethàwn nor ceremony was shown the Navajo here; but he was allowed to tarry four nights and was fed with an abundance of white corn meal and corn pollen.

58. Now Qastcèëlçi took him to a place called Lejpáhiço (Brown Earth Water) and led him to the top of a high hill, from which they could see in the far distance Gángiço, where the prophet's family dwelt; for they had moved away from the valley in Çepéntsa, where he left them. Then the yay showed him the shortest road to take and bade him return to his people.

59. When he got within sight of his house his people made him stop and told him not to approach nearer until they had summoned a Navajo shaman. When the latter, whose name was Red Queue, came, ceremonies were performed over the returned wanderer, and he was washed from head to foot and dried with corn meal; for thus do the Navajo treat all who return to their homes from captivity with another tribe, in order that all alien substances and influences may be removed from them. When he had been thus purified he entered the house and his people embraced him and wept over him. But to him the odors of the lodge were now intolerable and he soon left the house and sat outside. Seeing this, the shaman gave it as his opinion that the purification al-

ready made was not sufficient, and that it would be well to have a great dance over him. In those days the Navajo had a healing dance in the dark corral; but it was imperfect, with few songs and no kethàwns or sacrificial sticks. It was not until Dsilyi‘ Neyáni recounted his revelations that it became the great dance it now is among the Navajo.

60. It was agreed that before the dance began Dsilyi‘ Neyáni should be allowed four days and four nights in which to tell his story and that the medicine man should send out a number of young men to collect the plants that were necessary for the coming ceremony. For four nights and for four days he was busy in relating his adventures and instructing his hearers in all the mysteries he had learned in the homes of the ȼigìni. Then they built the medicine lodge and got all things ready for the new rites and for the purification of the one who had returned. The shaman selected from among the plants brought him by the young men such as he thought would best cleanse his patient of all the strange food he had taken among the alien Indians and in the houses of the supernatural ones whom he had visited. On the first day he gave him pine and spruce; on the second day, big and little willows; on the third day, a plant called litci and the aromatic sumac; on the fourth day, cedar and piñon. Of these the prophet drank cold and hot infusions in the morning by the fire.

61. During these four days the ceremonies which Dsilyi‘ Neyáni had introduced were in progress. On the fifth day it was proposed they should send out the akániuili (meal sprinkler) or courier to invite their neighbors to the great dance. There were two couriers to be sent: one was to go to the north, to a place called Ȼògojilá‘ (Much Grease Wood), to invite some friendly bands of Ute, some distant bands of Navajo, and some Jicarilla who dwelt there; the other was to go to the south, to Tse‘lakàï-silà (Where Two White Rocks Lie), to ask the Southern Apache, the White Mountain Apache, the Cohonino, and a tribe called Ȼildjèhe, to attend. To the camp in the north it was a journey of two days and two nights, and it would take the fleetest runner the same time to return. To the home of their neighbors in the south it was as far. As these long journeys must be made on foot and running, they could not find a single young man in the camp who would volunteer for the task. The men counseled about the difficulty all day and tried much persuasion on the youths, but none were found willing to make either journey.

62. As night approached an old woman entered the medicine lodge and said: " I will send my grandson as an akáninili." This old woman's lodge was not far from where the medicine lodge was built and all present knew her grandson well. Whenever they visited her lodge he was always lying on the ground asleep; they never saw him go abroad to hunt, and they all supposed him to be lazy and worthless; so when she made her offer they only looked at one another and laughed. She waited awhile, and getting no response she again offered the services of her grandson, only to provoke again laughter and significant looks.

A third and a fourth time she made her proposal, and then she said: "Why do you not at least answer me? I have said that I will let my grandson take your messages to one of these camps and you laugh at me and thank me not. Why is this?" Hearing her words, the chief medicine man, who came from a distant camp and did not know her, asked the men who were present who the woman was and what sort of a young man her grandson was; but again the men laughed and did not answer him either. He turned to the old woman and said: "Bring hither your grandson, that I may see him." The woman answered: "It is already late; the night is falling and the way is long. It is of no use for you to see him to-night; let us wait until the morning." "Very well," said the shaman; "bring him at dawn to-morrow." She left the lodge promising to do as she was bidden; and the moment she was gone the long suppressed merriment of the men broke forth. They all laughed inordinately, made many jokes about the lazy grandson, and told the medicine man that there was no use in sending such a person with the message when the best runners among them did not dare to undertake the journey. "He is too weak and lazy to hunt," said they; "he lives on seeds and never tastes flesh."

63. As soon as there was light enough in the morning to discern objects, a man who was looking out of the door of the medicine lodge cried out, "He comes," and those inside laughed and waited. Presently Tlà-¢esçìni (such was the name of the old woman's grandson) entered and sat down near the fire. All looked at him in astonishment. When last they saw him his hair was short and matted, as if it had not been combed or washed for three years, and his form was lean and bent. Now he appeared with thick glossy locks that fell below his knee; his limbs were large and firm looking; he held his head erect and walked like a youth of courage; and many said to one another, "This cannot be the same man." In a little while another young man named Indsiskàï (Radiating White Streaks), as fair and robust as the first, entered and sat down by the fire on the side opposite to where Tlà¢esçìni sat. The white earth and the charcoal for painting the akáninili were already prepared; so some of the young men in the lodge, when they beheld this pair of fine couriers, arose without a word of debate and began to paint the latter and to adorn their persons for the journey. When the toilet was done, the medicine man sent the couriers forth with many messages and injunctions and told them to blow on their whistles four times before they got out of hearing of the lodge. Tlà¢esçìni went to the north and Indsiskàï to the south, and they walked so slowly that all the spectators again laughed and made merry, and many said: "They will never reach the camps whither we have sent them." They passed out of sight just before the sun rose. Those who remained in camp prepared to amuse themselves. They cleared the ground for the game of nánjoj, and brought out their sticks and hoops. Some said: "We will have plenty of time for play before the couriers return." Others said: "At

yonder tree we saw Tlà¢esçìni last. I suppose if we went there now
we would find him asleep under it."

64. About the middle of the afternoon, while they were playing their
games, one looked to the north, and, at a distance, he saw one of the
messengers approaching them, and he cried out, "Here comes Tlà¢esçìni;
he has wakened from his sleep and is coming back for something to
eat." A moment later Indsiskàï was announced as approaching from
the south. They both reached the door of the medicine lodge at the
same time; but Tlà¢esçìni entered first, handed his bag to the medicine
man, and sat down in the same place where he sat when he entered
in the morning. Indsiskàï followed and, handing his bag to the shaman, sat down opposite his companion. Now, many who were without
thronged into the lodge to enjoy the sport, and they laughed and whispered among themselves; but the couriers were grave and silent, and,
while the medicine man opened the bags, they took off their ornaments
and washed the paint from their bodies. In the bag of Tlà¢esçìni were
found four ears of léjyipěj (corn baked in the husk underground). They
were still hot from the fire, and the shaman broke them into fragments
and passed the pieces around. From the bag of Indsiskàï two pieces of
noçá' (the hard sugar of the maguey), such as the Apache make, were
taken. When the young men had finished cleaning themselves, they
passed out in silence, without a glance for any one.

65. At nightfall they returned to the lodge, and entering, sat down
in the west, one on each side of the medicine man, and Tlà¢esçìni addressed him, saying: "When we came to the lodge this afternoon, we
did not give you an account of our journeys because the people who are
with you are fools, who laughed when we came home from the long
journey which they feared to undertake; but now we have come to tell
you our adventures. I," continued Tlà¢esçìni, "went to the north. On
my way I met another messenger who was traveling from a distant
camp to this one to call you all to a dance in a circle of branches of a
different kind from ours. When he learned my errand he tried to prevail
on me to return hither and put off our dance till another day, so that we
might attend their ceremony and that they in turn might attend ours;
but I refused, saying our people were in haste to complete their dance.
Then we exchanged bows and quivers as a sign to our people that we
had met and that what we would tell on our return was the truth.
You observe that the bow and quiver I have now are not those with
which I left this morning. We parted, and I kept on my way towards
the north. It was yet early in the day when I reached Çògojilá', where
the Jicarilla and friendly Ute were encamped. There I sprinkled
meal on the medicine man and gave him my message. When I arrived
they were just opening a pit in which they had roasted corn, and they
gave me the ears which I have brought home. They promised to be
here in our camp at the end of the third day, which will be the night
of our dance."

66. When Tlà¢esçìui had done speaking, Indsiskàï gave the following account of himself: " It was but a little while after sunrise when I reached Tse'lakàï-silà and entered the camps of the four tribes. In one they were just taking some noçá' out of a pit, and they gave me those pieces which I brought home. I entered the lodge of a medicine man in each tribe, scattered on him the sacred meal, and announced to him when our dance would take place. They all promised to be here with their people on the end of the third day, which will be on the night we hold our ceremony."

67. When the akáninilis came to tell their adventures to the medicine man, they were beautifully attired. They wore earrings and necklaces of turquoise, coral, and rare shells. They had on embroidered blankets of a kind we see no longer, but the gods wore them in the ancient days. They rustled like dry leaves. The blanket of one was black and that of the other was white. When they came out of the medicine lodge they went around among the huts and inclosures of those who were assembled, visiting the wives and the sweethearts of the silly men who had laughed at them in the morning; and everywhere the women smiled on the beautiful and well dressed youths. The next morning the men laughed and sneered at them no more, nor whispered in their presence, but glanced at them with sulky or shamefaced looks. During the day the akáninilis took part in the game of nánjoj with those who once jeered at them, and won many articles of great value.

68. On the afternoon of the third day following the one on which the akáninilis made their journeys, a great cloud of dust was observed on the northern horizon and a similar cloud was seen in the south. They grew greater and came nearer, and then the invited Indians began to arrive from both directions. They continued to come in groups until nightfall, when a great multitude had assembled to witness the dance. After the guests began to arrive the young men set to work to cut trees for the corral, and when the sun had set the building of the dark circle of branches began. While the young men were making the circle the old men were making speeches to the multitude, for the old men always love to talk when the young men are hard at work. It was the greatest corral that has ever been built in the Navajo country. It was as broad as from Cañon Bonito to "the Haystacks" (a distance of about six miles), yet the visiting tribes were so numerous that they filled the circle full. In the mean time the sounds of singing and of the drum were heard all around, for many different parties of dancers, who were to take part in the night's entertainment, were rehearsing.

69. There was some delay after the inclosure was finished before the first dancers made their appearance. A man entered the corral and made a speech begging the atsáleï, or first dancers, to hasten, as there were so many parties from a distance who wished to perform during the night. Soon after he had spoken, the two atsáleï who led in the dance of the great plumed arrow entered, and after them came six more, and

performed this healing dance over Dsilyi' Neyáni as it is performed to this day. (See paragraph 131.) When this was concluded various groups from among the strangers entered, one after another, and conducted their different alìlis, or shows, which the Navajo then learned and have since practiced when they sing their songs in the dark circle of branches.

70. When the dance began in the evening there was one of the invited tribes which, it was noticed, had not arrived. This was the Beqai, or Jicarilla. The Navajo asked the Ute where the missing ones were, and the Ute answered that they had passed the Jicarilla on the way; that the latter were coming, but had stopped to play a game of roulette, or ná^{n}joj, and were thus delayed. Shortly before dawn the Jicarilla came and entered the corral to exhibit their alili or show. It was a dance of the ná^{n}joj, for the wands and implements of the dance were the sticks and wheels used in playing that game.

71. During the night a chief of the Navajo, while walking through the crowd, observed the grandmother of Tlà¢esçìni sitting on the ground. He approached her and said: "Your grandson and his friend have done a great deed for us; they have made a long journey. Many doubted whether they had really made it until we saw the multitude gathering in our camp from the north and from the south in obedience to their summons. Now we know that they have spoken the truth. Tell me, I beg you, how they did this wonderful thing." She answered: "They are ¢igìni. My grandson for many years has risen early every morning and run all around Tsòtsil (Mount Taylor, or San Mateo) over and over again before sunrise. This is why the people have never seen him abroad during the day, but have seen him asleep in his hogán. Around the base of Tsòtsil are many tse'ná'djihi (heaps of sacrificial stones). These were all made by my grandson; he drops a stone on one of these piles every time he goes round the mountain."

72. When day began to dawn there were yet several parties who came prepared to give exhibitions, but had not had a chance; still, at the approach of day the ceremonies had to cease. At this time, before the visitors began to leave the corral, the Navajo chief who had spoken with the grandmother arose and addressed the assembly. He told them all he knew about the swift couriers and all the grandmother had told him. He remarked that there were yet many who could not believe that the young men had made the journey; so, to satisfy all, he proposed that within twelve days they should have a race between the two fleet akáninili around the base of Tsòtsil, if all would agree to reassemble to witness it, and he begged them to invite their neighbors of the Pueblo and other tribes to come with them. Then other chiefs arose to speak. In the end the proposition of the Navajo chief was agreed to. All promised to return within eleven days and decided that the race should take place on the morning following. Then they dispersed to their homes.

73. On the afternoon of the eleventh day, when they had reassembled according to their promises, the Navajo chief arose and addressed them. He invited the chiefs of the other tribes to come forward and complete the arrangements for the race. So the headmen all came together at the place where the Navajo was speaking, and, after some consultation, they agreed that the race should be around the peak of Tsòtsil, but not around the entire range of mountains. The Navajo separated themselves into one party and the alien tribes into another, the two parties standing at a little distance from one another. The aliens were given the first choice, and they chose Indsiskàï; therefore Tlà¢esçìni fell to the Navajo. Then the betting began. The stakes consisted of strings of coral, turquoise, and shell beads, of vessels of shells as large as the earthen basins of the Zuñi, of beautifully tanned buckskins, of dresses embroidered with colored porcupine quills, and of suits of armor made of several layers of buckskin. The warriors in those days wore such armor, but they wear it no longer. The beads and shells were laid in one pile; the buckskins, the embroidered dresses, and the armor in another; and the piles were of vast size.

74. The homes of these young men were at Kaç-sakà¢ tsé'çqa (Lone Juniper Standing Between Cliffs), now Cobero Cañon. There is seen to day a rock shaped like a Navajo hogán. It stands near the wagon road and not far from the town of the Mexicans (Cobero). This rock was once the hut where Tlà¢esçìni dwelt. Not far from it is another rock of similar appearance, which once was the home of Indsiskàï. For this reason the runners were started at the Lone Juniper. They ran towards the west and five of the fleetest runners among the assembled Indians set out at the same time to see how long they could keep up with them. By the time these five men had reached the spur of the mountain opposite Çòsaço (Hot Spring, Ojo de los Gallinos, San Rafael), the two champions were out of sight. Then the five turned back; but before they could return to the Lone Juniper the runners had got in and the race was decided. Tlà¢esçìni had won by about twice the length of his own body, and all the wagered wealth of the other nations passed into the hands of the Navajo.

75. When all was done the strangers were dissatisfied; they mourned over their losses and talked about the whole affair among themselves for a long time. Finally they decided to give the Navajo another challenge if the latter would agree to a longer racecourse, which should include all the foothills of the San Mateo range. The Navajo accepted the challenge and agreed to have the race at the end of another twelve days. Early on the eleventh day the strangers began to assemble from all quarters; they continued to arrive all day, and when night fell they were all in. Then the headmen addressed them, explaining all the conditions of the challenge and describing carefully the racecourse decided on. The betting did not run as high this time as before.

The Navajo bet only about one-half of what they won on the former race. Again they started the two runners, and in such time as you could just mark that the sun had moved, they were back at the goal; but this time Indsiskaï, the champion of the alien races, won by about the same distance as he had lost on the previous occasion.

76. Then the strangers were satisfied and said, "We will try no more. Many of our goods are still with the Navajo; but we have done well to rescue what we have." One of the wise men among them said, "Yes, you have done well, for had you lost the second race you would have lost with it the rain and the sunshine and all that makes life glad." It is because the Navajo won so much wealth on this occasion that they have been richer than the neighboring races ever since.

77. The ceremony cured Dsilyi' Neyáni of all his strange feelings and notions. The lodge of his people no longer smelled unpleasant to him. But often he would say, "I know I cannot be with you always, for the yays visit me nightly in my sleep. In my dreams I am once more among them, and they beg me to return to them."

78. From Lejpáhiço the family moved to Dsildjoltcín¢i (Mountain of Hatred). Thence they went to Tsinbiláhi (Woods on One Side), and from there to Tse'yuçáhia' (Standing Rock Above). In this place they encamped but one night, and next day they moved to ¢epè-aça¢ (Sheep Promontory), and went on to ¢epè ¢asi¢i (One Sheep Lying Down). Here again they camped for the night. Next day they traveled by Tse'atcàl-çali (Rock Cracked in Two) to Tcoyàjnaskíç (Hill Surrounded With Young Spruce Trees), to Nigàqokaï (White Ground), and to Tse'yistci¢ (Dipping Rocks, i. e., dipping strata), where they stopped to rest for the night. On the following day they journeyed to Çosakázi (Cold Water), in which place they encamped again.

79. When the morning came, Dsilyi' Neyáni said to his younger brother, "Let us go out and try to shoot some deer, so that we may make beça' (deer masks), such as we wore in ¢epéntsa, where we killed so many deer." The brothers departed on the hunt and came to a place called Dsil-líjin (Black Mountains), and they sat down on the side of the mountains looking towards Tsòtsil. As they sat there Dsilyi' Neyáni said, "Younger brother, behold the ¢igìni!" (holy ones); but the younger brother could see no one. Then he spoke again, "Farewell, younger brother! From the holy places the gods come for me. You will never see me again; but when the showers pass and the thunder peals, 'There,' you will say, 'is the voice of my elder brother,' and when the harvest comes, of the beautiful birds and grasshoppers you will say 'There is the ordering of my elder brother.'"

80. As he said these words he vanished. The younger brother looked all around, and seeing no one he started for his home. When he returned to his people he told them of the departure of Dsilyi' Neyáni, and they mourned as for one dead.

THE CEREMONIES OF DSILYÍDJE QAÇÀL.

81. It has been my lot to see portions of these ceremonies at various times. The most complete view I had of them was during a visit made to a place called Niqotlízi (Hard Earth), some twenty miles northwest from Fort Wingate, New Mexico, and just within the southern boundary of the Navajo Reservation. This was the only occasion when I obtained full access to the medicine lodge on the later days of the ceremonies and had an opportunity of observing the wonderful pictures on sand which are illustrated in color in the accompanying plates.

82. On October 21, 1884, when I arrived at this place, the patient for whose benefit the rites were celebrated and a few of her immediate relations were the only people encamped here. They occupied a single temporary shelter of brushwood, within a few paces of which I had a rude shelter erected for my own accommodation. The patient was a middleaged woman, who apparently suffered from no ailment whatever; she was stout, ruddy, cheerful, and did her full share of the household work every day; yet she was about to give away for these ceremonies sheep, horses, and other goods to the value of perhaps two hundred dollars. No ceremonies whatever were in progress when I came. Everything, so the Indians said, was waiting for the qaçàli. (Paragraph 2.) Some men were engaged in building a corral for the sheep that were to be slaughtered for the guests, and some old women were grinding corn to feast the men who were to work in the medicine lodge, which had been completed six days before.

83. This lodge was a simple conical structure of large, partly hewed piñon logs, set on end and inclined at an angle of about forty-five degrees, so as to join one another on top, where they formed the apex of the lodge. The circle of logs was incomplete in the east, where the openings for the door and the smoke hole were. A passage, or entry, about five feet high and three feet wide, led from the body of the lodge to the outer doorway, where some blankets hung as portières. The frame of logs was covered with sods and loose earth to keep out wind and rain. Internally, the lodge was eight feet in height under the apex of the cone and on an average twenty-five feet in diameter at the base. The diameter was increased at the east (to allow for the entry) and at the north. The irregularity in the circumference in the north was at first conjectured to be a mere accident; but in the ceremonies of the first night its use became apparent as affording a hiding place for the man dressed in evergreens. (Paragraph 96.)

84. THE FIRST FOUR DAYS' ceremonies in this case had been performed during the previous year. Such a division of the work is sometimes made, if more convenient for the patient and his friends, but usually all is done in nine consecutive days. These first days have less of interest than the others. Early each morning, before eating, all who desire, men and women, enter the medicine lodge, where, in a stifling

atmosphere, seated around a fire of dry wood of four different kinds—cedar, big willow, little willow, and spruce—they take the hot emetic infusion of fifteen different kinds of plants mixed together. A little sand is placed in front of each to receive the ejected material. After the emetic has acted the fire is removed, deposited some paces to the north of the lodge, and allowed to die out. Each devotee's pile of sand is then removed (beginning with that of the man who sat in the east and going round the circle) and deposited, one after another, in a line north of the sacred fire. Each succeeding day's deposits are placed farther and farther north in a continuous line. Next all return to the lodge, which has been allowed to cool; the shaman spits on each some medicine which has been mixed with hoar-frost and is supposed to cool. When all have left the lodge, a new fire of ordinary wood is kindled, and the kethàwns, or sacrificial sticks, appropriate to the day are made.

85. FIFTH DAY. The chanter did not arrive until the afternoon of October 23. His ceremonies in the medicine lodge began on the morning of the 24th. The forenoon was devoted to the preparation and sacrifice of certain kethàwns (keçàn)—the sacrificial sticks, to the origin of which so much of the foregoing myth is devoted—and of sacrificial cigarettes. About eight o'clock the sick woman entered the medicine lodge, followed by the chanter. While she sat on the ground, with her limbs extended, he applied some powdered substance from his medicine bag to the soles of her feet, to her knees, breasts, shoulders, cheeks, and head, in the order named, and then threw some of it towards the heavens through the smoke hole. Before applying it to the head he placed some of it in her mouth to be swallowed. Then, kneeling on a sheep skin, with her face to the east, and holding the bag of medicine in her hand, she recited a prayer, bit by bit, after the chanter. The prayer being finished, she arose, put some of the medicine into her mouth, some on her head, and took her seat in the south, while the shaman went on with the preparation of the sacrifices.

86. An assistant daubed a nice straight branch of cherry with some moistened herbaceous powder, after which he divided the branch into four pieces with a flint knife. Two of the pieces were each about two inches long and two each about four inches long. In each of the shorter ones he made one slight gash and in each of the longer ones two gashes. The sticks were then painted, a shred of yucca leaf being used for the brush, with rings of black, red, and white, disposed in a different order on each stick. The two cigarettes were made by filling sections of some hollow stem with a mixture of some pulverized plants. Such cigarettes are intended, as the prayers indicate, to be smoked by the gods. (Paragraph 88.)

87. While the assistants were painting the sticks and making the cigarettes the old chanter placed on a sheep skin, spread on the floor woolly side down, other things pertaining to the sacrifice: five bundles of assorted feathers, five small pieces of cotton sheeting to wrap the sacri-

fices in, and two round flat stones, each about four inches in diameter. The upper surfaces of these he painted, one blue and one black, and he bordered each with a stripe of red. When the kethàwns and cigarettes were ready, the qaçàli distributed them along with the bunches of plumes, on the five pieces of cotton cloth, which were then rolled up around their contents, making five bundles of sacrifices. On the completion of this work there was prayer, song, and rattling; the medicinal powder was applied to the body of the patient as before (paragraph 85); two of the little sacrificial bundles were placed in her right hand, and while she held them she again repeated a prayer, following again phrase by phrase, or sentence by sentence, the words of the priest. The latter, when the prayer was ended, took the sacrifices from her hand and pressed them to different parts of her body in the order previously observed, beginning with the soles of the feet and going upwards to the head, but on this occasion touching also the back, and touching it last. Each time after pressing the sacrifices to her body he held them up to the smoke hole and blew on them in that direction a quick puff, as if blowing away some evil influence which the sacrifices were supposed to draw from her body. Then the three remaining bundles were put in her hands and the rites observed with the former bundles were repeated in every respect, including the prayer, which was followed by singing and rattling. When the song had ceased some of the assistants took the bundles of sacrifices out of the lodge, no doubt to bury them according to the method proper for those particular kethàwns. The round painted stones were also carried out.

88. The prayers which the woman repeated varied but little. They all sounded nearly alike. The night the shaman arrived he rehearsed some of these prayers with the woman, at her own hogán, to make her familiar with them before she repeated them in the medicine lodge. The prayer addressed to Dsilyi‘ Neyáni, when she held in her hand the offering sacred to him, was as follows:

> Reared Within the Mountains!
> Lord of the Mountains!
> Young Man!
> Chieftain!
> I have made your sacrifice.
> I have prepared a smoke for you.
> My feet restore thou for me.
> My legs restore thou for me.
> My body restore thou for me.
> My mind restore thou for me.
> My voice restore thou for me.
> Restore all for me in beauty.
> Make beautiful all that is before me.
> Make beautiful all that is behind me.
> Make beautiful my words.
> It is done in beauty.
> It is done in beauty.
> It is done in beauty.
> It is done in beauty. (Paragraphs 261-4.)

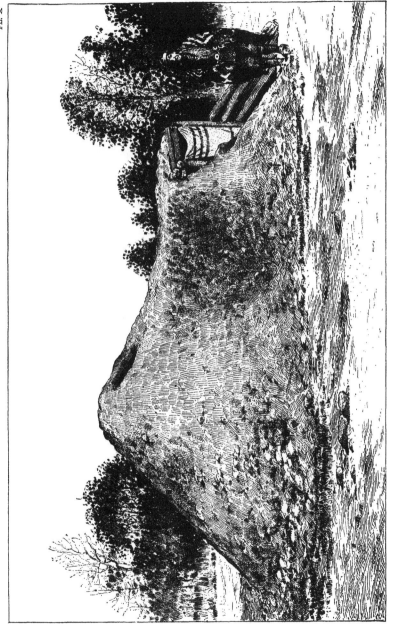

MEDICINE LODGE. VIEWED FROM THE SOUTH.

MEDICINE LODGE, VIEWED FROM THE EAST.

89. The next part of the ceremonies (or, shall I say, the treatment?) was a fumigation. The medicine man took from the fire a large glowing coal, placed it beside the woman, and scattered on it some powdered substance which instantly gave forth a dense smoke and a strong fragrance that filled the lodge. The woman held her face over the coal and inhaled the fumes with deep inspirations. When the smoke no longer rose the coal was quenched with water and carried out of the lodge by the chief, Manuelito, probably to be disposed of in some established manner. Then the woman left the lodge and singing and rattling were resumed.

90. While the rites just described were in progress some assistants were busy with other matters. One made, from the spotted skin of a fawn, two bags in which the akáninilis or couriers were to carry their meal on the morrow's journey. Another brought in and hung over the doorway a bundle of dry, withered plants which he had just gathered. Glancing up at them I recognized the *Gutierrezia* and the *Bouteloua*. The bundle may have contained the other plants mentioned in the myth (paragraph 44). They were hung up there till the next day, to be then used in a manner which will be described (paragraph 101).

91. The sheepskin on which the sacrifices had been placed was taken away and a blanket was spread on the ground to receive some more sacred articles from the bag of the chanter. These were five long notched wands, some tail feathers of the wild turkey, some small downy feathers of the eagle, and some native mineral pigments—yellow ocher, a ferruginous black, and a native blue. With the pigments the assistants painted the notched wands; with the plumes the chanter trimmed them. (See Fig. 51 and Plate XI.) Then they were called çobolçà, a word of obscure etymology, or inçia', which signifies sticking up or standing erect. They are called in this paper "plumed wands."

92. While some were making the çobolçà others busied themselves grinding, between stones, large quantities of pigments, coarser than those referred to above, to be used in making the sand pictures or dry paintings of the ceremony. They made five colors: black, of charcoal; white, of white sandstone; red, of red sandstone; yellow, of yellow sandstone; and "blue," of the black and white, mixed in proper proportions; of course this was a gray, but it was their only cheap substitute for the cerulean tint, and, combined with the other colors on the sanded floor, in the dim light of the lodge, it could not easily be distinguished from a true blue. It may be remarked in passing that the Navajo apply to many things which are gray the term they use for blue (çolíj); thus the gray fox is called màï-çolíj (blue coyote) and a gray sheep is called a blue sheep. Yet that they make a distinction between these colors is, I think, fairly evident from the fact that in painting small articles, such as kethàwns and masks, they use the more costly articles of turquoise, malachite, and indigo. These coarse pigments for the dry paintings were put for convenience on curved pieces of piñon bark.

From time to time, during this and the following days, as the heaps of colored powder diminished under the hands of the artists, more stones and charcoal were pulverized to replenish them.

93. About noon they cleared off that portion of the floor of the lodge which lay west of the fire, and brought, in blankets, a quantity of dry sand, which they spread out over the cleared portion of the floor in a layer of the nearly constant depth of three inches. They smoothed the surface with the broad oaken battens used in weaving. Now for a time all operations were suspended in the lodge while the chanter went out to plant the çobolçà, or plumed wands, in front of the medicine lodge, and to lay beside them the collars of beaver skins and the symbols for wings which the couriers were to wear next day. (Fig. 51.) These articles, it was said, were placed outside as a sign to the gods that the holy pictures were being drawn; but it is not improbable that they were intended also as a sign to uninitiated mortals. However that may be, they were taken in as soon as the picture was finished. The great painting was begun about 1 o'clock p. m., was finished about 3, and was allowed to remain until the ceremonies at night were concluded. It will be described later. (Paragraphs 160 et seq.)

FIG. 51. The çobolçà, or plumed wands, as seen from the door of the medicine lodge.

94. When the picture was completed food was brought in, and there was a good deal of eating and sleeping and smoking done. Being informed that nothing more would be done until after nightfall, I went to my own shelter, to elaborate some of my more hasty sketches while matters were still fresh in my mind. At 7 o'clock a messenger came to tell me that ceremonies were about to be resumed. During my absence the principal character in the night's performance — a man arrayed in evergreens — had been dressed.

95. I found, on returning to the lodge, a number of spectators seated around close to the edge of the apartment. The fire burned in the center. The sick woman, with some companions, sat in the south. The qaçàli, with a few assistants who joined him in singing and shaking rattles, was seated at the north, at the place where the circumference of the lodge was enlarged. (Paragraph 83.) There was a space about two feet wide and six feet long between them and the wall, or roof if you choose so to call it, of the lodge. I was assigned a place in the west. The sick woman was directed to move from the position she occupied

in the south, and sit, with her face to the east, at the junction of the two white serpents that cross one another on the picture. (Plate XV.)

96. When she was seated the qaçàli began a song, accompanied by the usual rattling and drumming. At a certain part of the song the chanter was seen to make a slight signal with his drumstick, a rapid stroke to the rear, when instantly a mass of animate evergreens—a moving tree, it seemed—sprang out from the space behind the singers and rushed towards the patient. A terrifying yell from the spectators greeted the apparition, when the man in green, acting as if frightened by the noise, retreated as quickly as he came, and in a moment nothing could be seen in the space behind the singers but the shifting shadows cast by the fire. He was so thoroughly covered with spruce twigs that nothing of his form save his toes could be distinguished when he rushed out in the full glare of the fire. This scene was repeated three times, at due intervals.

97. Some time after the third repetition, the chanter arose, without interrupting his song, and proceeded to erase the picture with his rattle. He began with the mountain in the west (paragraph 162), which he completely leveled; next in order he erased the track of the bear; next, the hole in the center; and then, one by one, the various other figures, ending with the serpents on the outside. In erasing the serpents, he began with the figures in the east and followed the apparent course of the sun, ending with the figures in the north. When the picture was completely obliterated, the sand on which it had been drawn was collected, put in a blanket, and carried out of doors, to be thrown away.

98. Then the sick woman was lifted by two other women and laid on her side where the picture had been, with her face to the east. While she lay there, the medicine man, amid much singing, walked around her, inscribed on the earth at her feet a straight line with his finger and erased it with his foot, inscribed at her head a cross and rubbed it out in the same manner, traced radiating lines in all directions from her body and obliterated them, gave her a light massage, whistled over her from head to foot and all around her, and whistled towards the smoke hole, as if whistling something away. These acts were performed in the order in which they are recorded. His last operation on her was a severe massage, in which he kneaded every part of her body forcibly and pulled her joints hard, whereat she groaned and made demonstrations of suffering. This concluded, she rose. A blanket was spread on the ground on the north of the fire, near where the man in evergreens was concealed. At the last appearance of the man in evergreens the woman fell back apparently paralyzed and suffering from difficulty of breathing, all of which was probably feigned, but was supposed to be a sign that the right remedy or ceremony for her ailment had been found and that none other need be tried. The medicine man now proceeded to restore her to consciousness by drawing zigzag lines from her body

east and west and straight lines north and south, like their symbols for the chain and sheet lightnings, by stepping over her in different directions, and by rattling. When she had apparently recovered, he pressed the plumed wands and the symbols for wings to different parts of her body, in the order and with the ceremonies described when referring to previous application made to her body.

99. There were no more ceremonies that night. I remained in the medicine lodge until it was quite late. The men occupied their time in singing, rattling, gambling, and smoking. After a while some grew weary and lay down to sleep. Being repeatedly assured that nothing more would happen until the whistle sounded in the morning, I left the lodge to roll myself in my blankets. Yet frequently during the night, fearing I might have been deceived, I stealthily arose and visited the medicine lodge, only to find all slumbering soundly.

FIG. 52. Akáninili ready for the journey.

100. SIXTH DAY. At five in the morning (Saturday, October 25) the whistle sounded and I hastened to the medicine lodge. There was much to be done; the couriers were to be dressed and sent on their way, and a large picture was to be painted; so the work had to begin early.

101. The first thing done was to burn to charcoal the bundle of plants which had been gathered on the previous morning and hung over the door of the lodge inside. (Paragraph 90.) The charcoal was used in painting the limbs of the akáninilis or couriers. A basin of water containing soap root or amolë (the root of *Yucca baccata* and other species of yucca) was brought in, and after the medicine man had dabbed them with a little of the suds the akáninilis-elect washed themselves with it from head to foot, cleaning their hair well. When the bath was done, they were dabbed by the qaçàli with some other mixture contained in a waterproof wicker basin and were made to inhale the fra-

grant fumes of some vegetable powder scattered on a live coal, which, as usual, was "put out," in a double sense, when the fumigation was over. Then the young men were dressed and adorned to look like Dsilyi' Neyáni after his toilet in the house of the butterflies. (Paragraph 44.) Their legs and forearms were painted black, to represent the storm cloud. The outer aspects of these members were decorated with white zigzag streaks, to indicate the white lightning. Their faces were painted partly white and small white spots were scattered over their bodies. Downy eagle feathers were fastened to their hair; necklaces of shell and coral were hung around their necks, and over these were laid collars of beaver skin, with whistles attached, which had lain in front of the lodge the day before, near the plumed wands. (Paragraph 93, Fig. 51.) Small objects to represent wings were tied to their arms. Each was given one of the fawn skin bags (paragraph 90) with corn meal in it. In the hand of the akáninili who was to go to the south was placed one of the çobolçà, or plumed wands, whose stem was painted black, the color of the north, as a sign to all he might meet that he was a duly authorized messenger from a medicine lodge in the north. In the hand of the other akáninili was placed a blue shafted wand, to show that he came from the south. Thus equipped they were all ready for the journey. (Fig. 52.)

102. The chanter gave them his messages, telling them where to go, what places they were to visit, what other chanters they were to see, what dancers they were to invite, and what gifts they were authorized to offer to the visiting performers for their trouble. Having given these special instructions, he closed with the general instructions, which are always given to the akáninili, as follows:

These [pointing to the eagle feathers on the head] will make for you a means of rising as you progress.

These [pointing to the wing symbols on the arm] will bear you onward.

This [pointing to the collar of beaver skin] will be a means of recognition for you. For this reason it hangs around your neck.

Sprinkle meal across a little valley, across a big arroyo.

Across the roots of a tree sprinkle meal and then you may step over.

Sprinkle meal across a flat rock.

Then the plumed wand. For this purpose you carry it, that they will recognize you as coming from a holy place.

103. The akáninili on his journey scatters meal before him as directed in these charges. He also scatters it on the medicine men whom he visits, and for this reason he is called akáninili, which signifies meal sprinkler.

104. When the last word of the instructions was uttered, the couriers departed, one to the north and one to the south. It was not later than 7 o'clock when they left. As soon as they were gone, the work of painting the picture appropriate to the day was begun. It was much more elaborate than the painting of the previous day. Although a dozen men worked on it, it was not finished until two o'clock. About the time

it was done, the akáninili from the south returned. He was carefully divested of all his ornaments. The white paint was scraped carefully from his body and preserved in the medicine bags of those who scraped it off. Then he was led out of the lodge.

105. When the picture was finished, the shaman, having applied pollen in three places to each god, stuck around it in the ground, at regular intervals, the three plumed wands which had stood before the door of the lodge all day and the wand which the akáninili from the south had just brought back with him. This wand he placed at the south of the picture, and laid beside it the collar, wings, and plumes which the akáninili had worn. The fifth, or north, wand was still absent with the courier who went to the north.

106. All was ready now for the treatment of the sick woma She was sent for, and a crier went to the door of the lodge to announce that song and ceremony were to begin. Accompanied by another woman, she entered, carrying a basket with corn meal in it. This she sprinkled lightly over the picture and then handed it to some of the assistants, who finished the work she had begun by strewing the meal plentifully on the figures. She sat on the form of the god in the east, facing the door, with her feet extended, and her companion sat on the figure of the cornstalk in the southeast. (Plate XVI.) In the mean time the medicine man had made a cold infusion in an earthen bowl and placed it on the hands of the rainbow figure (paragraph 169), laying over it a brush or sprinkler made of feathers, with a handle of colored yarn. When the women were seated, the chanter dipped his brush in the solution; sprinkled the picture plentifully; touched each divine figure with the moistened brush in three places — brow, mouth, and chest; administered the infusion to the women, in two alternate draughts to each; drained the bowl himself; and handed it to the bystanders, that they might finish the dregs and let none of the precious stuff go to waste. Next came the fumigation. The woman whom we have designated as the companion rose from her seat on the picture and sat on the ground beside the door. The principal patient retained her seat on the eastern god. Near each a live coal was laid on the ground. On the coal a strong scented but rather fragrant mixture was thrown, and as the fumes arose the women waved them towards their faces and breathed them in as before. The coal was extinguished and carefully removed, as on previous occasions. The application of the sacred dust to the body of the patient followed. The shaman moistened his hands with saliva and pressed them to the feet of all the gods. Some of the powder, of course, stuck to his palms. This he applied to the feet of the patient. Thus he took dust from the knees, abdomens, chests, shoulders, and heads of the figures and applied it to corresponding parts of the patient's form, making a strong massage with each application.

107. When the patient had departed many of the spectators advanced to the picture and gathered the corn pollen (paragraphs 105 and 112), now

rendered doubly sacred, and put it in their medicine bags. Some took portions of the remaining dust from the figures, after the manner of the shaman, and applied it to ailing portions of their persons. If the devotee had disease in his legs, he took dust from the legs of the figures; if in his head, the dust was taken from the heads of the figures, and so on.

108. By the time they were all done the picture was badly marred; yet its general form and some of the details were quite distinguishable. Then it became the province of the chanter to completely obliterate it. He began with the white god in the east and took in turn the figures in the southeast (corn), south, southwest, west, center, northwest, north, and northeast. Next, the figure of the rainbow was erased from foot to head, and, on his way, the chanter knocked down, with rather vicious blows, the plumed wands which stood up around the picture. When he came to the round figure in the center he dug up a cup which had been buried there. He erased the picture with a long slender wand and sang in the mean time, to the accompaniment of the rattling of his assistants, a plaintive chant in a minor key, which was perhaps the most melodious Indian song I ever heard. All was over at half past 2 in the afternoon.

109. Later in the day it was announced that the other akáninili was approaching from the north. He could then be observed about a mile away in an open plain. As he advanced the sound of his whistle was heard. At exactly half past 4 he entered the medicine lodge, where the chanter motioned him to a seat in the south. Singing and rattling were at once begun and the akáninili was divested of his trappings in the following order: head plumes, beaver collar, necklace, right wing, left wing, belt, sash, moccasins. The white paint was removed and preserved as on the former occasion. He was led out of the lodge, where he was well washed from head to foot in a hot decoction of the detergent amolë and dried with corn meal. Two large blood blisters were to be seen on the inner aspects of his thighs, brought on by the friction of his breechcloth in running. He said that he had run constantly when not in sight from our camp, had traveled a long way since morning, and was very tired. It seems to be the custom with the akáninilis to walk slowly when near camp and to run when out of sight, probably to follow the mythic examples of Tlá¢esçìni and Indsiskàï. (Paragraph 63.)

110. With the toilet of the akáninili the ceremonies of the day ended. He returned to the lodge to relate his adventures and get some food. During the day visitors arrived occasionally from distant camps. In the afternoon there were several young men present, who busied themselves in grubbing and clearing the ground where the corral was to be built and the great dance of the last night was to be held. I remained in the lodge until it was quite late, and I frequently rose during the night to see if anything was going on; but the night passed without event, like the previous one.

111. SEVENTH DAY. The painting of the picture and the treatment of the sick woman were the only works performed on this day (Sunday, October 26). The whistle sounded from the lodge at 6 a. m., but already the plumed wands and the beaver collars had been placed before the door of the medicine lodge and the sand for the groundwork of the picture had been brought in. As the picture (Plate XVII) was to be larger than those which preceded it, the fire was moved quite near to the door; the heated earth which lay under the fire in its former position was dug up and replaced with cold earth, probably for the comfort of the artists.

112. The work of the painters was begun soon after 6 a. m. and was not completed until about 2 p. m. About a dozen men were engaged on it, and it occupied them, as we have seen, about eight hours. As usual, the qaçàli did very little of the manual labor; but he constantly watched the work and frequently criticised and corrected it. When the painting was done, it became his duty to apply the sacred corn pollen to the brow, mouth, and chest of each of the gods and to set up the bounding çobolçà or plumed wands. After this he placed a bowl of water on the left hand of the white god—the form second from the north—threw into it some powdered substance to make a cold decoction, and laid the sprinkler on top of it. (Paragraph 106.)

113. The whistle was blown. The herald announced that all was ready. The sick woman and her companion entered, and one after the other cast meal upon the floor. The former took off her moccasins and sat on the ground near the door while a song was sung. Then she sat on the form of the white god, her companion sat on the form of the blue god, and the singing and rattling were resumed. Without interrupting his song the chanter sprinkled the picture with the infusion, applied the moistened sprinkler to the breast, head, and brow of each of the gods in the following order: white, blue, yellow, black, and sat down to finish his chant. He administered the decoctions to his patient in two draughts, to her companion in two draughts, to himself (honest physician!) in the same manner, and gave as before (paragraph 106) the dregs to the bystanders. He applied the dust from different parts of the divine figures to the sick woman, in much the same manner as on the previous day, and while doing this he obliterated the pictures of the little animals over the head of the white god. The fumigation of both women was repeated with exactly the same rites as on the second day, and the fumes had precisely the same odor on this occasion as on that. When the coals were extinguished and taken out, the chanter said to the women, "kaç" (now), whereat they arose and left the lodge.

114. As soon as they were gone the work of obliteration began. The figures of the gods were rubbed out in the usual order (white, blue, yellow, black, rainbow), the erasure in each case proceeding from foot to head. The plumed wands fell as before, simultaneously with the destruction of the rainbow. The sand was carried out at half past 2 o'clock and no further rites were performed during the day.

115. EIGHTH DAY. The picture painted on Monday (October 27) was of a simple character, and hence did not occupy much time. The work was begun at 7 a. m. and was finished at 10 a. m. Of the four shorter or interior arrows (Plate XVIII), that which stands second from the north was regarded as the arrow of the east and was begun first. On this arrow the sick woman was placed, sitting with her face to the east, when she came to be treated and fumigated. The bowl of infusion was laid on the point of the arrow immediately to her left, regarded as the arrow of the north. The medicine man put the pollen on the base, on the red cross lines near the center, and on the white tips. All the ceremonies which took place between the completion and the obliteration of the picture (the planting of the five plumed wands, the sprinkling of the picture with meal, the sprinkling and administration of the infusion, the application of the colored dust to the person of the patient, the fumigation of the two women, the whistling, the singing, and rattling) were essentially the same as those observed on the previous day. In taking the dust from the picture, however, the shaman applied his hands only to the bases of the arrows. The ceremony of obliteration was also a repetition of the rites of the previous day.

116. The building of the great stack of wood (Fig. 53) which was to furnish the fire in the center of the corral on the last night went on

FIG. 53. The great wood pile.

simultaneously with the painting of the picture. Both tasks were begun and ended about the same time. The wood in the big pile was dead, long seasoned juniper and cedar, fuel of the most inflammable character. The pile was about twelve feet high and sixty paces in circumference. Large quantities of this dry wood were also brought and placed outside the space allotted to the corral, to replenish the fires when needed.

117. In the afternoon there were no ceremonies in the medicine lodge. The qaçàli and his assistants took a half holiday, and not without deserving it, for they had wrought well for three days and they had a long day's work and a long night's work still before them. A large number of people had by this time assembled, and from time to time more arrived. Throughout the sparse grove which surrounded us, little temporary corrals and huts of boughs were going up in every direction. In more secret spots in the rugged walls of a cañon, about half a mile from the medicine lodge, other shelters were erected, where visiting performers were to prepare themselves on the last night. Many young men were busy in the afternoon cutting down the trees and lopping off the branches which were to form the great corral (the ilnásjin, the dark circle of branches) on the next day. Some of the visiting women were busy grinding meal and attending to different household duties; others played cards or engaged in the more aboriginal pastime of áz¢ilçil, a game played with three sticks and forty stones, the latter for counters.

118. The friends of the sick woman prepared the alkàn, a great corn cake baked in the earth, the manufacture of which gave evidence of the antiquity of the process. The batter was mixed in one large hole in the ground lined with fresh sheepskin. It was baked in another hole in which a fire had been burning for many hours, until the surrounding earth was well heated. The fire was removed; the hole lined with corn husks; the batter ladled in and covered with more cornhusks; hot earth and hot coals were spread over all. The cake was not dug up until the following day, and was designed chiefly for the special entertainment of those who were at work in the medicine lodge.

119. NINTH DAY (UNTIL SUNSET). On Tuesday (October 28) the work in the lodge consisted in preparing certain properties to be used in the ceremonies of the night. These were the wands to be used in the first dance, the kátso-yisçàn or great plumed arrows, and the trees which the dancers pretended to swallow.

120. The wand of the nahikàï was made by paring down a straight slender stick of aromatic sumac, about three feet long, to the general thickness of less than half an inch, but leaving a head or button at one end. A ring was fashioned from a transverse slice of some hollow or pithy plant, so that it would slide freely up and down the slender wand, but would not pass over the head. Eagle down was secured to the wooden head and also to the ring. In the dance (paragraph 129) the eagle down on the stick is burned off in the fire while the ring is held in the palm of the hand. When the time comes for the wand to grow white again, as the name nahikàï expresses it, the ring is allowed to leave the palm and slide to the other end of the stick.

121. The great plumed arrows were deceptions somewhat similar in character to the wands. One-half of the arrow was made of a slender

hard twig of cliff rose; the other half was formed of some pithy suf-fruticose herb which I could not determine satisfactorily, as I saw only the cut sections and was not permitted to handle these. The pith was removed so as to allow the wooden part to move into the herby part with a telescopic mechanism. The herbaceous portion was so covered with feathers that nothing could be seen of its surface. A large stone arrowhead was attached to the wooden shaft. When the actor pre-tended to swallow this he merely held the stone point firmly between his teeth and forced the upper or plumed shaft down on the lower or wooden shaft. It was an excellent deception, and presented to the or-dinary observer all the appearance of genuine arrow swallowing.

122. The piñon saplings, which the dancers also pretended to swallow, had no deceptive arrangement. They were slender little trees trimmed at the butt into a broad, thin, wedge shaped point, which was carefully smoothed by rubbing it with sandstone, so that no offensive splinters should present themselves to the lips of the dancers. The smooth end was painted red, probably to make the spectators, at night, by the un-certain firelight, suppose that the dissemblers had torn their throats in their great efforts. Sometimes the saplings have all their branches removed, and are then trimmed with cross pieces and circles of ever-green sprays. In most cases, however, I have seen the sapling used in its natural condition.

123. As each set of implements was completed there was a ceremony with singing and rattling, the men who were to use them at night partook of powdered medicines on their extended tongues, from the hands of the chanter, and then practiced themselves in the use of the implements. Although they well knew the deceptive nature of these articles and fully understood the frauds they were preparing to per-petrate on the public, these young men seemed to view the whole work with high reverence and treat it with the greatest seriousness. For instance, when, in the secrecy of the lodge, they went through the motions of swallowing the trees they showed indubitable signs of fear: all looked anxious, some trembled quite perceptibly, and one looked as pale as a live Indian can look. They probably dreaded the displeasure of the gods if all were not done well.

124. LAST NIGHT. Just after sunset the old chanter posted himself some paces to the east of the great woodpile, on the spot where the gate of the corral was to be, and began a song. Simultaneous with the begin-ning of the song was the commencement of the building of the dark circle. All the young and middleaged men in camp assisted. They dragged the branches from where they had been cut down in the neigh-boring woods and put them in position in the circle with great celerity. The work was all done in less than an hour, during which time the chanter ceased not for an instant his song and rattle. When the fence was finished to his satisfaction he stopped his song and the labors of the workmen ceased with the sound. When finished the corral averaged

about forty paces in diameter, and the fence was about eight feet high, with an opening left in the east about ten feet wide.

125. The moment the dark circle of branches was finished it inclosed sacred ground. Any dog who dared to enter was chased out with shouts and missiles. The man or woman who came must, on the first occasion, pass around to the left, i. e., to the south of the great wood-pile. No one was allowed to peep through the fence or look over the edge of it to witness the ceremonies. That part of the auditorium was reserved for the spirits of the bears and other ancestral animal gods. No horse might be led into the inclosure until after sunrise next morning, when the fence was razed and all became common soil once more.

126. When the night began to fall many of the visitors moved all their goods into the corral and lighted there a number of small fires close to the fence, temporarily abandoning their huts and shelters outside. Those who did not move in left watchers to protect their property; for there are thieves among the Navajo. The woods around the corral were lighted up in various directions by the fires of those who had not taken their property into the great inclosure and of parties who were practicing dances and shows of an exoteric character.

127. The nocturnal performances of *this* evening (Tuesday, October 28, 1884) were as meager as any I have seen within the dark circle of branches. The best show I ever witnessed in the circle was one which took place at Keam's Cañon, Arizona, on the 5th of November, 1882. For this reason I will make the notes taken on the latter occasion the basis of my description of the " corral dance," adding as I proceed such comments as may be justified by subsequent observation and information.

128. At 8 o'clock a band of musicians which I will call the orchestra entered, sat down beside one of the small fires in the west, and began to make various vocal and instrumental noises of a musical character, which continued with scarcely any interruption until the close of the dance in the morning. At the moment the music began the great central fire was lighted, and the conflagration spread so rapidly through the entire pile that in a few moments it was enveloped in great flames. A storm of sparks flew upward to the height of a hundred feet or more, and the descending ashes fell in the corral like a light shower of snow. The heat was soon so intense that in the remotest parts of the inclosure it was necessary for one to screen his face when he looked towards the fire. And now all was ready to test the endurance of the dancers who must expose, or seem to expose (paragraph 149), their naked breasts to the torrid glow.

129. *First dance* (Plate XII). When the fire gave out its most intense heat, a warning whistle was heard in the outer darkness, and a dozen forms, lithe and lean, dressed only in the narrow white breech-cloth and moccasins, and daubed with white earth until they seemed a group of living marbles, came bounding through the entrance, yelping

like wolves and slowly moving around the fire. As they advanced in single file they threw their bodies into divers attitudes — some graceful, some strained and difficult, some menacing. Now they faced the east, now the south, the west, the north, bearing aloft their slender wands tipped with eagle down, holding and waving them with surprising effects. Their course around the fire was to the left, i. e., from the east to the west, by way of the south, and back again to the east by way of the north, a course taken by all the dancers of the night, the order never being reversed. When they had encircled the fire twice they began to thrust their wands toward it, and it soon became evident that their object was to burn off the tips of eagle down; but owing to the intensity of the heat it was difficult to accomplish this, or at least they acted well the part of striving against such difficulty. One would dash wildly towards the fire and retreat; another would lie as close to the ground as a frightened lizard and endeavor to wriggle himself up to the fire; others sought to catch on their wands the sparks flying in the air. One approached the flaming mass, suddenly threw himself on his back with his head to the fire, and swiftly thrust his wand into the flames. Many were the unsuccessful attempts; but, at length, one by one, they all succeeded in burning the downy balls from the ends of their wands. As each accomplished this feat it became his next duty to restore the ball of down. The mechanism of this trick has been described (paragraph 120), but the dancer feigned to produce the wonderful result by merely waving his wand up and down as he continued to run around the fire. When he succeeded he held his wand up in triumph, yelped, and rushed out of the corral. The last man pretended to have great difficulty in restoring the down. When at last he gave his triumphant yell and departed it was ten minutes to 9. The dance had lasted twenty minutes.

130. In other repetitions of this ceremony the writer has witnessed more of burlesque than on this occasion. Sometimes the performers have worn immense false mustaches, exaggerated imitations of spectacles and of other belongings of their white neighbors. Sometimes the dance has assumed a character which will not be described in this place (paragraph 146). It is called nahikàï-alil. The former word signifies "it becomes white again" and refers to the reappearance of the eagle down. The show is said to have been introduced among the Navajo at the great corral dance mentioned in the myth (paragraphs 69–72) by a tribe from the south named Çildjèhe. It is no essential part of the rites of the dark circle, yet I have never known it to be omitted, probably because it is a most suitable dance for the time when the fire is the hottest.

131. *Second dance.* After an interval of three-quarters of an hour, the dance of the kátso-yisçàn, the great plumed arrow, the potent healing ceremony of the night, began. There were but two performers. They were dressed and arrayed much like the akáninili, but they bore no meal bags, wore no beaver collars, and the parts of their bodies that

were not painted black—legs and forearms—were daubed with white earth. Instead of the wand of the akáninili, each bore in his hand one of the great plumed arrows. While they were making the usual circuits around the fire, the patient (a man on this occasion) was placed sitting on a buffalo robe in front of the orchestra. They halted before the pa-

FIG. 54. Dancer holding up the great plumed arrow.

FIG. 55. Dancer "swallowing" the great plumed arrow.

tient; each dancer seized his arrow between his thumb and forefinger about eight inches from the tip, held the arrow up to view, giving a coyote-like yelp, as if to say, "So far will I swallow it" (Fig. 54), and then appeared to thrust the arrow, slowly and painfully, down his throat (Fig. 55) as far as indicated. While the arrows seemed still to be stuck in their throats, they danced a chassé, right and left, with short, shuffling

DANCE OF NAHIKÁI.

PL. XII

FIRE DANCE.

PL. XIII.

steps. Then they withdrew the arrows, and held them up to view as before, with triumphant yelps, as if to say, "So far have I swallowed it." Sympathizers in the audience yelped in response. The next thing to be done was to apply the arrows. One of the dancers advanced to the patient, and to the soles of the feet of the latter he pressed the magic weapon with its point to the right, and again with its point to the left. In a similar manner he treated the knees, hands, abdomen, back, shoulders, crown, and mouth in the order named, giving three coyote-like yelps after each application. When the first dancer had completed the work, the other took his place and went through exactly the same performance. This finished, the sick man and the buffalo robe were removed. The bearers of the arrows danced once more around the fire and departed.

132. The plumed arrow is frequently referred to in the songs of this rite. It seems to be the most revered implement and the act in which it appears the most revered alili of the night. All the other shows may be omitted at will, but the dance of the kátso-yisçàn, it is said, must never be neglected. I have witnessed other performances where the arrow swallowers reappeared with their numbers increased to six or eight. The additional dancers all pretended to swallow arrows, but they did not apply them to the patient. The origin of this alili is well accounted for in the myth (paragraphs 47, 55, and 69), and the peculiar significance of the injunction not to break the arrow is easily understood when we know how the arrow is made.

133. *Third dance.* At 10 o'clock the sound of the whistle again called the spectators to attention and a line of twenty-three dancers came in sight. The one who led the procession bore in his hand a whizzer (Fig. 56) such as schoolboys use, a stick tied to the end of a string; this he constantly whirled, producing a sound like that of a rain storm. After him came one who represented a character, the Yèbaka (anglicized, Yaybaka), from the great nine days' ceremony of the klèdji-qaçàl, or night chant, and he wore a blue buckskin mask that belongs to the character referred to. From time to time he gave the peculiar hoot or call of the Yàybichy, "hu‘hu‘hu‘hu" (paragraph 32). After him followed eight wand bearers. They were dressed like the bearers of the great plumed arrows; but instead of an arrow each bore a wand made of grass, cactus, and eagle plumes. The rest of the band were choristers in ordinary dress. As they were all proceeding round the fire for the fourth time they halted in the west, the choristers sat and the standing wand bearers formed a double row of four. Then the Yaybaka began to hoot, the orchestra to play, the choristers to sing, the whizzer to make his mimic storm, and the wand bearers to dance. The latter, keeping perfect time with the orchestra, went through a series of figures not unlike those of a modern quadrille. In our terpsichorean nomenclature the "calls" might have thus been given: "Forward and back. Chassez twice. Face partners. Forward and back. Forward and bow. Forward and embrace. Forward and wave wands at part-

ners, " &c. When several of these evolutions had been performed in a graceful and orderly manner, the choristers rose, and all went singing out at the east.

134. Three times more the same band returned. In the third and fourth acts the wands were exchanged for great piñon poles (eight to ten feet long), portions of which they pretended to swallow, as their predecessors had done with the arrows. (Paragraph 48.) That the simple and devoted Pueblo Indian does actually, in dances of this character, thrust a stick far down his gullet, to the great danger of health and even of life, there is little reason to doubt; but the wily Navajo attempts no such prodigies of deglutition. A careful observation of their movements on the first occasion convinced me that the stick never passed below the fauces, and subsequent experience in the medicine lodge only strengthened the conviction (paragraph 121).

135. The instrument designated above as the whizzer is a thin, flat, pointed piece of wood, painted black and sparkling with the specular

Section.

iron ore which is sprinkled on the surface; three small pieces of turquoise are inlaid in the wood to represent eyes and mouth. One whizzer which I examined was nine inches long, one and three-fourths inches broad, and about a quarter of an inch thick in the thickest part. (Fig. 56.) To it was attached a string about two feet long, by means of which the centrifugal motion was imparted to it. It is called by the Navajo tsín-ɖe‘ní‘, or groaning stick. It is used among many tribes of the southwest in their ceremonies. The Navajo chanters say that the sacred groaning stick may only be made of the wood of a pine tree which has been struck by lightning.

136. In the *Fourth dance* there were about thirty choristers, in ordinary dress, bearing piñon wands; there was a man who shook a rattle, another who whirled the groaning stick, and there were three principal dancers, wearing fancy masks and representing characters from the rites of the klèdji qaçàl or dance of the " Yàybichy." These three danced a lively and graceful jig, in perfect time to the music, with many bows, waving of wands, simultaneous evolutions, and other pretty motions which might have graced the spectacular drama of a metropolitan theater. Three times they left the corral for a moment, and returning varied the dance, and always varied to improve. The wands they bore were large light frames of reeds adorned with large eagle plumes.

FIG. 56. The whizzer.

137. After this there was an interval of nearly an hour, which passed slowly with those in the corral. Some smoked and gossiped; some listened to the never ceasing din of the orchestra or

THE DARK CIRCLE OF BRANCHES AT SUNRISE.

joined in the chant; some brought in wood and replenished the waning fires; some, wrapped in their serapes, stretched themselves on the ground to catch short naps.

138. *Fifth dance.* It was after midnight when the blowing of a hoarse buffalo horn announced the approach of those who were to perform the fifth dance, the tcòhanoai alili or sun show. There were twenty-four choristers and a rattler. There were two character dancers, who were arrayed, like so many others, in little clothing and much paint. Their heads and arms were adorned with plumes of the war eagle, their necks with rich necklaces of genuine coral, their waists with valuable silver studded belts, and their loins with bright sashes of crimson silk. One bore on his back a round disk, nine inches in diameter, decorated with radiating eagle plumes to represent the sun. The other carried a disk, six and a half inches in diameter, similarly ornamented, to symbolize the moon. Each bore a skeleton wand of reeds that reminded one of the frame of a great kite; it was ornamented with pendant eagle plumes that swayed with every motion of the dancer. While the whole party was passing round the fire in the usual manner wands were waved and heads bowed towards the flames. When it stopped in the west the choristers sat and sang and the rattler stood and rattled, while the bearers of the sun and the moon danced at a lively rate for just three minutes. Then the choristers rose and all sang and danced themselves out of sight. A second performance of this dance came between the first and second repetitions of the next show.

139. I have recorded one story (but have heard of another) accounting for the origin of this dance; it is as follows: When Dsílyi' Neyáni visited the mountain of Bistcàgi, the home of Estsàn Çigìni, these divine beings had for ornaments on their walls the sun and the moon. When the great mythic dance was given they were among the guests. They brought their wall decorations, and when the time for their alili came. they wore the sun and the moon on their backs when they danced.

140. The *Sixth dance,* that of the standing arcs, was both picturesque and ingenious. The principal performers were eight in number, as usual with scanty clothing. Their hair fell loose and long over back and shoulders and each bore in front of him, held by both hands, a wooden arc, ornamented with eagle plumes. The ends of the arc (which was a full semicircle) showed tufts of piñon twigs, and they were evidently joined together by a slender string, which was invisible to the audience. Besides the eight principal actors, there was a rattler, a bearer of the groaning stick, and a chorus. While all were making the fourth circuit of the fire, frequent shouts of "Çòhe! Çòhe!" (Englished, Thòhay—"Stand! stand!" or "Stay! stay!") were heard, the significance of which soon became apparent. When they stopped in the west, the eight character dancers first went through various quadrille-like figures, such as were witnessed in the third dance, and then knelt in two rows that faced one another. At a word from the rattler the man who was nearest to him

(whom I will call No. 1) arose, advanced to the man who knelt opposite to him (No. 2) with rapid, shuffling steps, and amid a chorus of "Thòhay! Thòhay!" placed his arc with caution upon the head of the latter. Although it was held in position by the friction of the piñon tufts at each ear and by the pressure of the ends of the arc, now drawn closer by the sub-tending string, it had the appearance of standing on the head without material support, and it is probable that many of the uninitiated believed that only the magic influence of the oft-repeated word "Thòhay" kept it in position. When the arc was secured in its place, No. 1 retreated with shuffling steps to his former position and fell on his knees again. Immediately No. 2 advanced and placed the arc which he held in his hand on the head of No. 1. Thus each in turn placed his arc on the head of the one who knelt opposite to him until all wore their beautiful halo-like headdresses. Then, holding their heads rigidly erect, lest their arcs should fall, the eight kneeling figures began a splendid, well timed chant, which was accentuated by the clapping of hands and joined in by the chorus. When the chant was done the rattler addressed the arc bearers, warning them to be careful; so they cautiously arose from their knees and shuffled with stiffened spines out of the corral, preceded by the choristers. This dance was repeated after the second performance of the fifth dance.

141. *Seventh dance.* The arc bearers had scarcely disappeared when another troupe entered the circle, the buffalo horn announcing their coming. A man with a whizzer led the procession. The choristers, in ordinary dress, were thirteen in number. The principal dancers were but two; they wore the usual sash and belt; the uncovered skin was painted white; they had on long blue woolen stockings of Navajo make and moccasins. Each bore a slender wand of two triangles of reeds, adorned at the corners with pendant plumes. They saluted the fire as they danced around it. They halted in the west, where the choristers sat down, and the two wand bearers danced for three minutes in a lively and graceful manner, to the music of the whizzer, the rattle, the choristers, and the drum of the orchestra. These returned twice more, making some variation in their performance each time. In the second act the rattler brought in under his arm a basket containing yucca leaves, and a prayer was said to the sun. It is possible that this dance was but a preliminary part of the eighth dance, but it must be described as a separate alili.

142. *Eighth dance.* In this there were sixteen performers, in ordinary Navajo dress. One of these bore the whizzer and led the procession; another, who came in the center of the line, carried a hewn plank, or puncheon, about 12 feet long and 4 inches broad, painted with spots and decorated with tufts of piñon branchlets and with eagle plumes; immediately behind the bearer of the plank walked a man who had in a basket an effigy of the sun, formed of a small round mirror and a number of radiating scarlet plumes. Having walked around the fire as usual,

the whole party gathered in the west in a close circle, which completely excluded from the sight of the audience the operations of the actors. Singing, rattling, and cries of "Thòhay!" were heard. In a few minutes the circle opened and the hewn plank, standing upright on a small Navajo blanket, without any apparent prop or support, was disclosed to view. At the base of the plank was the basket holding the figure of the sun. Singing was continued and so were the uproarious cries of "Thòhay"— cries anxious, cries appealing, cries commanding—while the bearer of the rattle stood facing the pole and rattling vigorously at it. At length, seemingly in obedience to all this clamor, the solar image left the basket and slowly, falteringly, totteringly, ascended the plank to within a few inches of the top. Here it stopped a moment and then descended in the same manner in which it rose. Once more was it made to rise and set, when the circle of dancers again closed, the plank, sun, and basket were taken in custody, and the dancers departed. Taking into consideration the limited knowledge and rude implements of the originators (for this alili is not of modern origin), this was a well performed trick. The means used for supporting the pole and pulling up the sun could not be detected. The dancers formed a semicircle nearly ten feet distant from the pole and the light of the central fire shone brightly upon all.

143. *Ninth dance.* It was after 1 o'clock in the morning when the dance of the hoshkàwn (*Yucca baccata*) began. (Fig. 57. See paragraph 3.) The ceremony was conducted in the first part by twenty-two persons in ordinary dress. One bore, exposed to view, a natural root of yucca, crowned with its cluster of root leaves, which remain green all winter. The rest bore in their hands wands of piñon. What other properties they may have had concealed under their blankets the reader will soon be able to conjecture. On their third journey around the fire they halted in the west and formed a close circle for the purpose of concealing their operations, such as was made in the eighth dance. After a minute spent in singing and many repetitions of "Thòhay," the circle opened, disclosing to our view the yucca root planted in the sand. Again the circle closed; again the song, the rattle, and the chorus of "Thòhay" were heard, and when the circle was opened the second time an excellent counterfeit of the small budding flower stalk was seen amid the fascicle of leaves. A third time the dancers formed their ring of occultation; after the song and din had continued for a few seconds the circle parted for the third time, when, all out of season, the great panicle of creamy yucca flowers gleamed in the firelight. The previous transformations of the yucca had been greeted with approving shouts and laughter; the blossoms were hailed with storms of applause. For the fourth and last time the circle closed, and when again it opened the blossoms had disappeared and the great, dark green fruit hung in abundance from the pedicels. When the last transformation was completed the dancers

went once more around the fire and departed, leaving the fruitful yucca behind them.

144. In a moment after they had disappeared the form of one personating an aged, stupid, short sighted, decrepit man was seen to emerge slowly from among the crowd of spectators in the east. He was dressed in an old and woefully ragged suit and wore a high, pointed

Fig. 57. Yucca baccata.

hat. His face was whitened and he bore a short, crooked, wooden bow and a few crooked, ill made arrows. His mere appearance provoked the "stoic" audience to screams of laughter, and his subsequent "low comedy business," which excelled much that I have seen on the civilized stage, failed not to meet with uproarious demonstrations of approval. Slowly advancing as he enacted his part, he in time reached the place where the yucca stood, and, in his imbecile totterings, he at length stumbled on the plant and pretended to have his flesh lacerated by the sharp leaves. He gave a tremulous cry of pain, rubbed saliva on the part supposed to be wounded, and muttered his complaints in a weak and shaking voice. He pretended then to seek for the plant, and was three times wounded in his efforts to find it. At length, kneeling on the ground, with his face buried in the leaves, he feigned to discover it, and rejoiced with querulous extravagance over his success. When he had marked the spot and the way back to it with an exaggerated burlesque of the Indian methods of doing these things, he went off to find his "old woman" and bring her to pick the fruit. Soon he returned with a tall, stalwart man, dressed to represent a hideous, absurd looking old granny. The latter acted his part throughout the rest of the drama with a skill fully equal to that of his comrade.

145. There were scenes in this drama which may not be told in this connection. It will suffice to say here that when the yucca fruit was picked and put in the basket the old man helped the "woman" to shoulder her load and the pair left the corral. The hackàn-inçá' does not invariably appear in the corral dance. I have attended one ceremony where it was omitted. I have heard two descriptions of the dance which differed very much from the one given above.

146. Many facts concerning not only the hackàn inçá', but other parts of the mountain chant, have not been allowed to appear in this essay. Recognized scientists may learn of them by addressing the author through the Director of the Bureau of Ethnology.

147. *Tenth dance.* At twenty minutes past three an uninteresting performance called the "bear dance" began. A man entered on all fours; his face was painted white; he wore around his loins and over his shoulders pieces of some dark pelt which may have been bear skin, but looked more like the skin of a black sheep. The fire had now burned low and the light was dim. He was accompanied by two attendants, one of whom carried a rattle. He went twice around the ring, imitating the lumbering gait of the bear. He occasionally made a clumsy lunge sidewise at some of the spectators, as though he would attack them; but on these occasions the man with the rattle headed him off and rattling in his face directed him back to the usual course around the fire. This show lasted five minutes.

148. The *Eleventh dance* was the fire dance, or fire play, which was the most picturesque and startling of all. Some time before the actors entered, we heard, mingled with the blowing of the buffalo horn, strange sounds, much like the call of the sand-hill crane; they will, for convenience, be called trumpeting. These sounds continued to grow louder and come nearer until they were heard at the opening in the east, and in a second after, ten men, having no more clothing on than the performers in the first dance, entered. Every man except the leader bore a long thick bundle of shredded cedar bark in each hand and one had

two extra bundles on his shoulders for the later use of the leader. The latter carried four small fagots of the same material in his hands. Four times they all danced around the fire, waving their bundles of bark towards it. They halted in the east; the leader advanced towards the central fire, lighted one of his fagots, and trumpeting loudly threw it to the east over the fence of the corral. He performed a similar act at the south, at the west, and at the north ; but before the northern brand was thrown he lighted with it the bark bundles of his comrades. As each brand disappeared over the fence some of the spectators blew into their hands and made a motion as if tossing some substance after the departing flame. When the fascicles were all lighted the whole band began a wild race around the fire. At first they kept close together and spat upon one another some substance of supposed medicinal virtue. Soon they scattered and ran apparently without concert, the rapid racing causing the brands to throw out long brilliant streamers of flame over the hands and arms of the dancers. Then they proceeded to apply the brands to their own nude bodies and to the bodies of their comrades in front of them, no man ever once turning round ; at times the dancer struck his victim vigorous blows with his flaming wand; again he seized the flame as if it were a sponge and, keeping close to the one pursued, rubbed the back of the latter for several moments, as if he were bathing him. In the mean time the sufferer would perhaps catch up with some one in front of him and in turn bathe him in flame. At times when a dancer found no one in front of him he proceeded to sponge his own back, and might keep this up while making two or three circuits around the fire or until he caught up with some one else. At each application of the blaze the loud trumpeting was heard, and it often seemed as if a great flock of cranes was winging its way overhead southward through the darkness. If a brand became extinguished it was lighted again in the central fire; but when it was so far consumed as to be no longer held conveniently in the hand, the dancer dropped it and rushed, trumpeting, out of the corral. Thus, one by one, they all departed. When they were gone many of the spectators came forward, picked up some of the fallen fragments of cedar bark, lighted them, and bathed their hands in the flames as a charm against the evil effects of fire.

149. Did these dancers, next day, hide sore and blistered backs under their serapes ? I think not, for I have seen and conversed with some of the performers immediately after the fire show, and they seemed happy and had nothing to complain of. Did the medicine they spat on one another save them? Certainly not, although the Indians claim it is a true prophylactic against burns and call it azè sakázi or cold medicine. But it is probable that the cedar bark ignites at a low temperature, and more than probable that the coating of white earth with which their bodies were covered is an excellent non-conductor. However, the thought that their bodies might have been thus ingeniously protected lessened little, if any, the effect produced on the spectator. I

have seen many fire scenes on the stage, many acts of fire eating and fire handling by civilized jugglers, and many fire dances by other Indian tribes, but nothing quite comparable to this in all its scenic effects.

150. The closing ceremonies I did not witness on this occasion, but I saw them at subsequent dances. Shortly before sunrise an assistant passed around the fire four times and sprinkled a little water on the mass of smoldering embers, while the medicine man chanted the appropriate song. Later, three gaps were torn in the circle of branches— one in the south, one in the west, and one in the north—making, with the original gate in the east, four entrances to the corral. (See Plate XIV.) Just after sunrise the entire circle of branches was razed, but the branches were not carried away. The traveler through the Navajo country often encounters withered remains of these circles. In the ceremony of October, 1884, the chanter, having another engagement which was pressing, packed up his sacred utensils and left soon after sunrise. The patient, it was said, was not permitted to sleep until after sunset.

151. *Other dances.* In subsequent dances I saw exhibitions which did not occur in the ceremony of November 5, 1882, just described, and I have learned of other shows produced on the last night, which I have never had an opportunity to witness. All the alilis may be modified. I have rarely seen two performances of the same dance which were just alike.

152. On two occasions I have witnessed a very pretty dance, in which an eagle plume was stuck upright in a basket and by means of some well hidden mechanism caused to dance in good time to the song, the beat of the drum, and the motions of the single Indian who danced at the same time; not only this, but the feather followed the motions of the Indian: if he danced toward the north, the feather leaned to the north while making its rhythmical motions; if he moved to the south, it bent its white head in the same direction, and so on. On one occasion it was a little boy, five years old, son of the chief Manuelito, who danced with the eagle plume. He was dressed and painted much like the akániuili, or the arrow swallowers (Figs. 54, 55), on a diminutive scale. The sash of scarlet velvet around his hips was beautifully trimmed with feathers. They said he had been several weeks in training for the dance, and he certainly went through his varied motions with great skill. I have rarely seen a terpsichorean spectacle that struck my fancy more than that of the little Indian child and his partner, the eagle plume.

153. It might be thought that the word "thóhay," so often used to make inanimate objects pay attention, was one of very sacred import. So it is, no doubt; yet I have seen it broadly burlesqued. It was on the occasion of the last "chant" which I attended. A number of boys, from twelve to fifteen years of age they seemed, led by a pleasant looking old man

with a skeptical twinkle in his eye, came into the dark circle. One of the party carried a deep Indian basket, from the top of which a number of spruce twigs protruded. They formed what has been designated as the ring of occultation, and while doing so they shouted and screamed and puffed the talismanic "thòhay" in a way that left no doubt of their intention to ridicule. Their extravagant motions added to the significance of their intonation. When the ring opened the boys sat on the ground and began to sing and beat a drum. The old man sat at a distance of about three paces west of the basket. Presently the nose of a little weasel (the image being probably a stuffed skin) appeared among the spruce boughs. All the timid, inquiring motions of the little animal were well mimicked: the nose was thrust forward and pulled back, the whole head would emerge and retreat, and at rare times the shoulders would be seen for a moment, to be quickly drawn in among the screening spruce twigs. All these motions were made in perfect time to the singing and drumming. The old man who pulled the actuating strings made no secret of his manipulations. The play was intended for a farce, and as such the spectators enjoyed it.

THE GREAT PICTURES OF DSILYÍDJE QAÇÀL.

154. A description of the four great pictures drawn in these ceremonies has been deferred until all might be described together. Their relations to one another rendered this the most desirable course to pursue. The preparation of the ground and of the colors, the application of the sacred pollen, and some other matters have been already considered.

155. The men who do the greater part of the actual work of painting, under the guidance of the chanter, have been initiated, but need not be skilled medicine men or even aspirants to the craft of the shaman. A certain ceremony of initiation has been performed on them four times, each time during the course of a different dance, before they are admitted into the lodge during the progress of the work or allowed to assist in it. The medicine man receives a good present in horses for his work; the assistants get nothing but their food. This, however, is abundant. Three times a day the person for whose benefit the dance is performed sends in enough mush, corn cake, soup, and roasted mutton to satisfy to the utmost the appetites of all in the lodge. There are some young men who live well all winter by going around the country from dance to dance and assisting in the work of the lodge.

156. The pictures are drawn according to an exact system. The shaman is frequently seen correcting the workmen and making them erase and revise their work. In certain well defined instances the artist is allowed to indulge his individual fancy. This is the case with the gaudy embroidered pouches which the gods carry at the waist. Within reasonable bounds the artist may give his god just as handsome a pouch

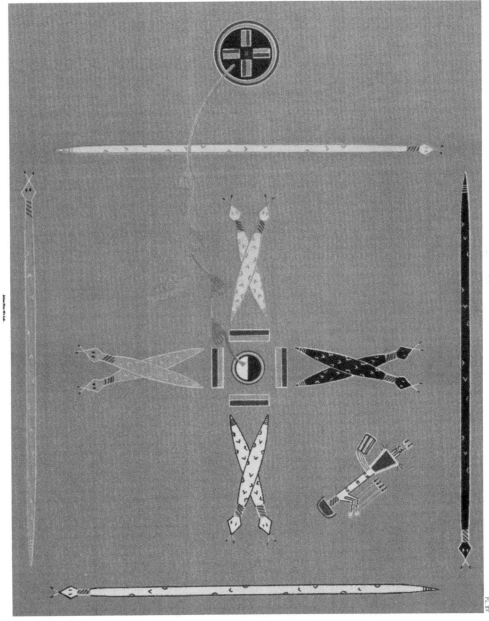

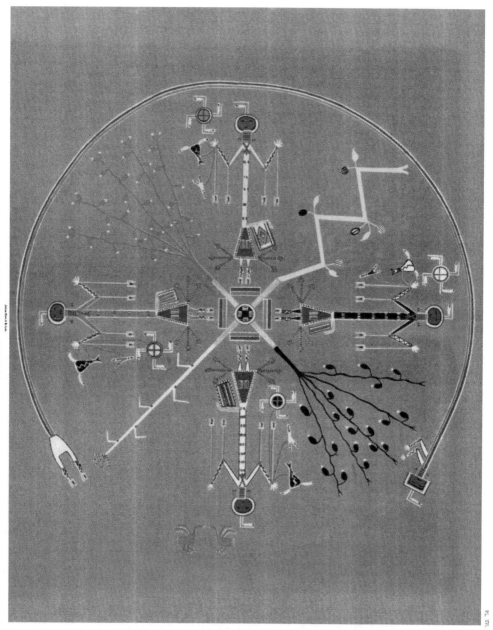

THIRD DRY PAINTING

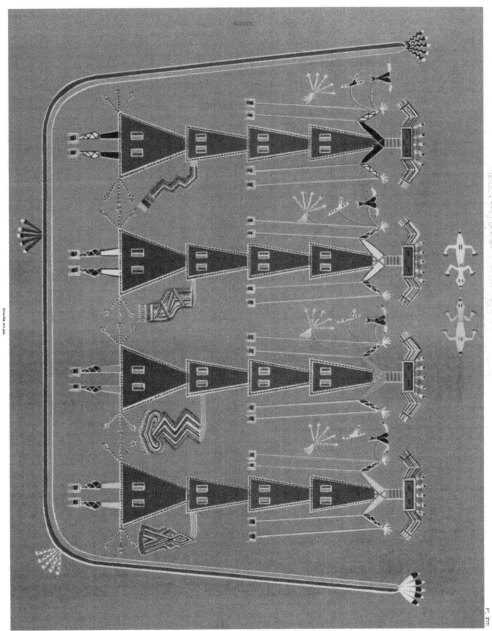

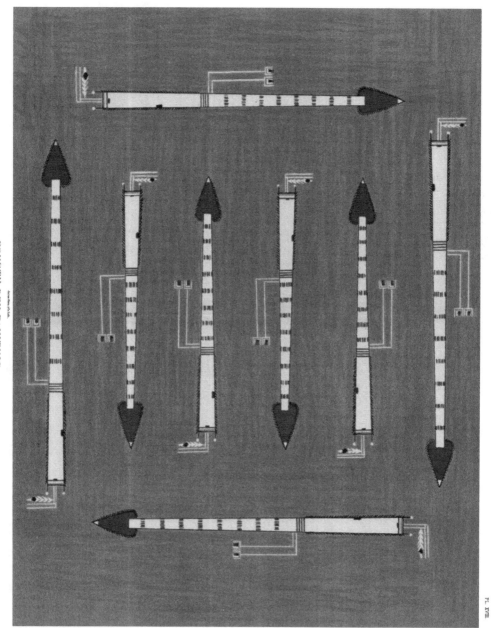

as he wishes. Some parts of the figures, on the other hand, are meas-
ured by palms and spans, and not a line of the sacred design can be
varied. Straight and parallel lines are drawn by aid of a tightened cord.
The mode of applying the colored powder is peculiar. The artist has
his bark trays laid on the sand where they are convenient of access. He
takes a small quantity of the powder in his closed palm and allows it to
pass out between his thumb and forefinger, while the former is moved
across the latter. When he makes a mistake he does not brush away
the pigment. He obliterates it by pouring sand on it, and then draws
the corrected design on the new surface. The forms of the gods do not
appear as I have represented them in the first coat of color. The naked
figures of these mythical beings are first completely and accurately
drawn and then the clothing is put on. Even in the pictures of the
"Long-bodies" (Plate XVII), which are drawn 9 feet in length, the
naked body is first made in its appropriate color—white for the east,
blue for the south, yellow for the west, and black for the north—and
then the four red shirts are painted on from thigh to axilla, as shown in
the picture.

157. The drawings are, as a rule, begun as much towards the center
as the nature of the figure will permit, due regard being paid to the
order of precedence of the points of the compass, the figure in the
east being begun first, that in the south next, that in the west third in
order, and that in the north fourth. The periphery is finished last of
all. The reason for thus working from within outwards is that the men
employed on the picture disturb the smooth surface of the sand with
their feet. If they proceed in the order described they can smooth the
sand as they advance and need not cross the finished portions of the
picture.

158. I have learned of seventeen great healing dances of the Navajo
in which pictures of this character are drawn. There are said to be,
with few exceptions—only one exception that I am positively aware of—
four pictures appropriate to each dance. Some of the dances are practiced somewhat differently by different schools or orders among the
medicine men, and in these divers forms the pictures, although agreeing
in general design, vary somewhat in detail. Thus there are, on an average, probably more than four designs, belonging to each of the seventeen
ceremonies, whose names I have obtained. If there were but four to
each, this would give us sixty-eight such paintings known to the medicine men of the tribe, and thus we may form some conception of the
great number of these sacred pictures which they possess. But I have
reason to believe, from many things I have heard, that besides these
seventeen great nine days' ceremonies to which I refer, there are many
minor ceremonies, with their appropriate pictures; so that the number
is probably greater than that which I give.

159. These pictures, the medicine men aver, are transmitted from
teacher to pupil in each order and for each ceremony unaltered from

year to year and from generation to generation. That such is strictly
the case I cannot believe. There are no standard pictures on hand
anywhere. No permanent design for reference is ever in existence,
and there is, so far as I can learn, no final authority in the tribe to settle
any disputes that may arise. Few of these great ceremonies can be
performed in the summer months. Most of the figures are therefore
carried over from winter to winter in the memories of fallible men. But
this much I do credit, that any innovations which may creep into their
work are unintentional and that if changes occur they are wrought
very slowly. The shamans and their faithful followers believe, or pro-
fess to believe, that the direst vengeance of the gods would visit them
if these rites were varied in the least in picture, prayer, song, or ceremonial. The mere fact that there are different schools among the
medicine men may be regarded as an evidence that changes have occurred.

160. FIRST PICTURE. The picture of the first day (Plate XV) is
said to represent the visit of Dsilyi' Neyáni to the home of the snakes
at Qoȼestsò. (Paragraph 53.)

161. In the center of the picture was a circular concavity, about six
inches in diameter, intended to represent water, presumably the house
of water mentioned in the myth. In all the other pictures where water
was represented a small bowl was actually sunk in the ground and
filled with water, which water was afterwards sprinkled with powdered
charcoal to give the impression of a flat, dry surface. Why the bowl
of water was omitted in this picture I do not know, but a medicine
man of a different fraternity from that of the one who drew the picture informed me that with men of his school the bowl filled with water
was used in the snake picture as well as in the others. Closely surrounding this central depression are four parallelograms about four
inches by ten inches in the original pictures. The half nearer the center
is red; the outer half is blue; they are bordered with narrow lines of
white. The same figures are repeated in other paintings. They appear
in this drawing, and frequently in others, as something on which the
gods seem to stand. They are the ca'bitlòl, or rafts of sunbeam, the
favorite vessels on which the divine ones navigate the upper deep. In
the Navajo myths, when a god has a particularly long and speedy
journey to make, he takes two sunbeams and, placing them side by side,
is borne off in a twinkling whither he wills. Red is the color proper
to sunlight in their symbolism, but the red and blue together represent
sunbeams in the morning and evening skies when they show an alter-
nation of blue and red. It will be seen later that the sunbeam shafts,
the halo, and the rainbow are represented by the same colors. In form,
however, the halo is circular, and the rainbow is distinguished by its
curvature, and it is usually anthropomorphic, while the sunbeam and
the halo are not. External to these sunbeam rafts, and represented as
standing on them, are the figures of eight serpents, two white ones in

the east, two blue ones in the south, two yellow ones in the west, and two black ones in the north. These snakes cross one another (in pairs) so as to form four figures like the letter **X**. In drawing these **X**'s the snake which appears to be beneath is made first complete in every respect, and then the other snake is drawn over it in conformity with their realistic laws of art before referred to. The neck, in all cases, is blue, crossed with four bands of red. The necks of the gods in all the pictures, it will be observed, are made thus, but the bars in the manlike figures run transversely, while those in the snake-like run diagonally. Three rows of **V**-shaped figures, four in each row, are seen on the backs of the snakes; these are simply to represent mottlings. Outside of these eight snakes are four more of much greater length; they form a frame or boundary to the picture, except in the west, where the mountain of Dsilyà-içín lies beyond them. There is a white snake in the east, lying from north to south and bounding the picture in the east; a blue snake, of similar size and shape, in the south; a yellow one in the west, and a black one in the north. They seem as if following one another around the picture in the direction of the sun's apparent course, the head of the east snake approximating the tail of the south snake, and so on.

162. In the northeast is seen the yay, Niltci, who accompanied the Navajo prophet to the home of the snakes. In the extreme west is a black circular figure representing the mountain of Dsilyà-içín. In the original picture the mountain was in relief—which I have not attempted to represent—a little mound of about ten or twelve inches high. The description of the mountain given in the myth is duly symbolized in the picture, the halo added. The green spot in the center is designed to represent a twig of spruce which was stuck in the mound of sand to indicate the spruce tree door. From the summit of the mountain to the middle of the central waters is drawn a wide line in corn meal, with four footprints, depicted at intervals, in the same material. This represents the track of a bear. Immediately south of this track is the figure of an animal drawn in gray pigment. This is the grizzly himself, which here, I have reason to believe, is used as a symbol of the Navajo prophet. The bear, in the sacred language of the shamans, is appropriately called Dsilyi' Neyáni, since he is truly reared within the mountains. His track, being represented by a streak of meal, has reference to the same thing as the name akáninili and the practice of the couriers (paragraph 102), who are dressed to represent the prophet, throwing corn meal in front of them when they travel.

163. The SECOND PICTURE is said to be a representation of the painting which the prophet saw in the home of the bears in the Carrizo Mountains (paragraph 40). In the center of this figure is the bowl of water covered with black powder, to which I referred before. The edge of the bowl is adorned with sunbeams, and external to it are the four ca'bitlol, or sunbeam rafts, on which seem to stand four gods, or yays.

164. The divine forms are shaped alike but colored differently. They lie with heads extended outward, one to each of the four cardinal points of the compass, the faces looking forward, the arms half extended on either side, with the hands raised to a level with the shoulders. They wear around their loins skirts of red sunlight, adorned with sunbeams. They have ear pendants, bracelets, and armlets, blue and red (of turquoise and coral), the prehistoric and emblematic jewels of the Navajo. Their forearms and legs are black, showing in each a zigzag mark to represent lightning on the surface of the black rain clouds. In the north god these colors are, for artistic reasons, reversed. Each bears, attached to his right hand with a string, a rattle, a charm, and a basket. The rattle is of the shape of those used by the medicine men in this particular dance, made of raw hide and painted to symbolize the rain cloud and lightning. The left hand is empty; but beside each one is a highly conventionalized picture of a plant. The left hand remains empty, as it were, to grasp this plant, to indicate that the plant at the left hand belongs to the god whose corresponding hand is unoccupied and extended towards it. The proprietorship of each god in his own particular plant is further indicated by making the plant the same color as the god. The body of the eastern god is white; so is the stalk of corn at his left, in the southeast. The body of the southern god is blue; so is the beanstalk beside him, in the southwest. The body of the western god is yellow; so is his pumpkin vine, in the northwest. The body of the north god is black; so is the tobacco plant, which is under his special protection, in the northeast.

165. Each of the four sacred plants is represented as growing from five white roots in the central waters and spreading outwards to the periphery of the picture. The gods form one cross whose limbs are directed to the four cardinal points; the plants form another cross having a common center with the first named cross, but whose limbs extend to the intermediate points of the compass.

166. On the head of each yay is an eagle plume lying horizontally and pointing to the right. A similar arrangement of four plumes, all pointing in one direction (contrary to the sun's apparent course), may be observed on the baskets carried by the gods.

167. The gods are represented with beautiful embroidered pouches, each of a different pattern. In old days the most beautiful things in art the Navajo knew of were the porcupine quill embroideries of the northern races. The art of garnishing with quills, and later with beads, seems never to have been practiced to any extent by the Navajo women. They obtained embroideries of the Ute and other northern tribes, and their ancient legends abound in allusions to the great esteem in which they held them. (See, for instance, paragraphs 32, 34.) Hence, to represent the grandeur and potency of their gods, they adorn them with these beautiful and much coveted articles.

168. Surrounding the picture on about three-fourths of its circum. ference is the anthropomorphic rainbow or rainbow deity. It consists of two long stripes, each about two inches wide in the original picture, one of blue, one of red, bordered and separated by narrow lines of white. At the southeastern end of the bow is a representation of the body below the waist, such as the other gods have, consisting of pouch, skirt, legs, and feet. At the northeastern end we have head, neck, and arms. The head of the rainbow is rectangular, while the heads of the other forms in this picture are round. In the pictures of the Yàybichy dance we frequently observe the same difference in the heads. Some are rectangular, some are round; the former are females, the latter males; and whenever any of these gods are represented, by characters, in a dance, those who enact the females wear square stiff masks, like our dominoes, while those who enact the males wear roundish, baglike masks, of soft skin, that completely envelop the head. The rainbow god in all these pictures wears the rectangular mask. Iris, therefore, is with the Navajo as well as with the Greeks a goddess.

169. All the other gods bear something in their hands, while the hands of the rainbow are empty. This is not without intention. When the person for whose benefit the rites are performed is brought in to be prayed and sung over, the sacred potion is brewed in a bowl, which is placed on the outstretched hands of the rainbow while the ceremony is in progress and only taken from these hands when the draught is to be administered. Therefore the hands are disengaged, that they may hold the gourd and its contents when the time comes (paragraph 106).

170. In the east, where the picture is not inclosed by the rainbow, we see the forms of two birds standing with wings outstretched, facing one another, their beaks close together. These represent certain birds of blue plumage called by the Navajo çòli (*Sialia arctica*). This blue-bird is of the color of the south and of the upper regions. He is the herald of the morning. His call of "çòli, çòli" is the first that is heard when the gray dawn approaches. Therefore is he sacred, and his feathers form a component part of nearly all the plume sticks used in the worship of this people. Two bluebirds, it is said, stand guard at the door of the house wherein these gods dwell; hence they are repre-sented in the east of the picture.

171. Here is an appropriate occasion to speak of a part of Navajo symbolism in color to which reference has already several times been made. In the majority of cases the east is represented by white, the south by blue, the west by yellow, the north by black; the upper world by blue and the lower by a mixture of white and black in spots. The colors of the south and west seem to be permanent: the south is always blue and the west is always yellow, as far as I can learn; but the colors of the east and north are interchangeable. The cases are rare where white is assigned to the north and black to the east; but such cases

occur, and perhaps in each instance merit special study. Again, black represents the male and blue the female.

172. The THIRD PICTURE commemorates the visit of Dsilyi‘ Neyáni to Çaçò‘-behogan, or "Lodge of Dew" (paragraph 56). To indicate the great height of the Bitsès-ninéz the figures are twice the length of any in the other pictures, except the rainbows, and each is clothed in four garments, one above the other, for no one garment, they say, can be made long enough to cover such giant forms. Their heads all point to the east, instead of pointing in different directions, as in the other pictures. The Navajo relate, as already told (paragraph 56), that this is in obedience to a divine mandate; but probably there is a more practical reason, which is this: if they had the cruciform arrangement there would not be room on the floor of the lodge for the figures and at the same time for the shaman, assistants, and spectators. Economy of space is essential; but, although drawn nearly parallel to one another, the proper order of the cardinal points is not lost sight of. The form immediately north of the center of the picture is done first, in white, and represents the east. That immediately next to it on the south comes second in order, is painted in blue, and represents the south. The one next below that is in yellow, and depicts the goddess who stood in the west of the House of Dew-Drops. The figure in the extreme north is drawn last of all, in black, and belongs to the north. As I have stated before, these bodies are first made naked and afterwards clothed. The exposed chests, arms, and thighs display the colors of which the entire bodies were originally composed. The glòï (weasel, *Putorius*) is sacred to these goddesses. Two of these creatures are shown in the east, guarding the entrance to the lodge. The append-ages at the sides of the heads of the goddesses represent the glòï-bitcà, or headdresses of glòï skins of different colors which these mythic per-sonages are said to wear. Each one bears attached to her right hand a rattle and a charm, or plume stick, such as the gods in the second picture carry; but, instead of the basket shown before, we see a con-ventionalized representation of a branch of choke cherry in blossom; this consists of five diverging stems in blue, five roots, and five cruci-form blossoms in white. The choke cherry is a sacred tree, a mountain plant; its wood is used in making certain sacrificial plume sticks and certain implements of the dance; it is often mentioned in the songs of this particular rite. Some other adjuncts of this picture—the red robes embroidered with sunbeams, the arms and legs clothed with clouds and lightning, the pendants from the arms, the blue and red armlets, bracelets, and garters—have already been described when speaking of the second picture. The object in the left hand is a wand of spruce.

173. The rainbow which incloses the picture on three sides is not the anthropomorphic rainbow. It has no head, neck, arms, or lower ex-tremities. Five white eagle plumes adorn its southeastern extremity. Five tail plumes of some blue bird decorate the bend in the southwest.

The plumes of the red shafted flicker (*Colaptes auratus* var. *mexicanus*) are near the bend in the northwest and the tail of the magpie termi- nates the northeastern extremity. Throughout the myth, it will be remembered, not only is the House of Dew-Drops spoken of as adorned with hangings and festoons of rainbows, but many of the holy dwell- ings are thus embellished.

174. The FOURTH PICTURE represents the kátso-yisçàn, or great plumed arrows. These arrows are the especial great mystery, the potent healing charm of this dance. The picture is supposed to be a fac simile of a representation of these weapons, shown to the prophet when he visited the abode of the Tsilkè-ḍigìni, or young men gods, where he first saw the arrows (paragraph 47). There are eight arrows. Four are in the center, lying parallel to one another — two pointing east and two others, alternate, pointing west. The picture is bordered by the other four, which have the same relative positions and directions as the bounding serpents in the first picture. The shafts are all of the same white tint, no attention being paid to the colors of the cardinal points; yet in drawing and erasing the picture the cardinal points are duly hon- ored. Among the central arrows, the second from the top, or north margin of the design, is that of the east; it is drawn and erased first. The next below it is the arrow of the south; the third is that of the west. The one on top belongs to the north; it is drawn and erased last. The heads are painted red to represent the red stone points used; the fringed margins show the irregularities of their edges. The plumes at the butt are indicated, as are also the strings by which the plumes are tied on and the notches to receive the bowstring.

175. The ground of this picture is crossed with nebulous black streaks. These were originally present in all the pictures. I have omitted them in all but this, lest they might obscure the details of the reduced copies. It has been explained to me (although in the myth it is expressly stated only in one case, paragraph 40) that all these pictures were drawn by the gods upon the clouds and thus were shown to the Navajo prophet. Men cannot paint on the clouds, but according to the divine mandate they do the best they can on sand, and then sprinkle the sand with charcoal, in the manner indicated, to represent the cloudy scrolls where- on the primal designs of the celestial artists were painted.

SACRIFICES OF DSILYÍDJE QAÇÀL.

176. The sacrifices made to the gods during these ceremonies consist of nothing more than a few sticks and feathers, with the occasional addition of strings and beads — a form of sacrificial offering common among various tribes of the Southwest, including the sedentary Indians of the pueblos. During the six days' work in the medicine lodge and the corral, I saw but one lot of these sticks prepared (paragraphs 86, 87); but I think this lot represented two sets, i. e., sacrifices to two different

mythical beings.   It is, however, indicated in the myth that a considerable number of these sacrifices, called by the Navajo keçàn (Englished,
kethàwn), belong to the mountain chant and may properly be offered
during its celebration.   I have seen among the Navajo a few varieties
of these devotional offerings and I have obtained descriptions of many.
Although I cannot rely on the minute accuracy of these descriptions, I
will present them for such value as they may possess in illustrating
the general character of this system of worship, a system which might
profitably occupy for years the best labors of an earnest student to
elucidate.

177. Fig. 58 represents a kethàwn belonging, not to the mountain
chant, but to the klèdji-qaçàl, or chant of the night.   It is sacred to the
Youth and the Maiden of the Rock Crystal,
divine beings who dwell in Tsisnàtcini, a
great mountain north of the Pueblo of Jemez.
The original is in the National Museum at
Washington.   It consists of two sticks coated
with white earth and joined by a cotton
string a yard long, which is tied to each stick

by a clove hitch.   A
black bead is on the cen-
ter of the string; a tur-
key feather and an eagle
feather are secured with
the clove hitch to one of
the sticks.

178. Fig. 59 depicts a
kethàwn pertaining also
to the klèdji-qaçàl.   It
is called keçàn-yalçì‘, or
talking kethàwn.   The
sticks are willow.   The
one to the left is painted
black, to represent a male
character (Qastcèbaka)
in the myth and ceremo-
ny of klèdji-qaçàl.   The
other stick is painted
blue, to denote a female
character (Qastcèbaäd)
in the same rites.   The

FIG. 58. Sacrificial sticks
(keçàn).

blue stick has a diagonal
facet at the top to indicate

FIG. 59. The talking kethàwn
(keçàn-yalcì‘).

the square topped female mask (paragraph 168).   The naturally round
end of the black stick sufficiently indicates the round male mask.   The
cord wrapped around the two sticks is similar to that described in the

paragraph immediately preceding. About the middle of the cord is a long white shell bead, shown in the cut. The breast feathers of the turkey and the downy feathers of the eagle are attached to the sticks. This kethàwn I saw once in the possession of a Navajo qaçàli. I was permitted to sketch it, but could not purchase it. The interpretation given of its symbolism is that of the qaçàli who owned it. In the myth of klèdji-qaçàl it is said that the beneficent god Qastcèëlçi used this kethàwn when he removed from the prophet Co the evil spell which had been cast on the latter by the wind god.

179. In Schoolcraft's Archives of Aboriginal Knowledge, Philadelphia, 1860, Vol. III, page 306, is a cut illustrating an article undoubtedly of a similar nature to that shown in Fig. 59. It is a sacrificial plume stick of the Moki. The Moki interpreter explained to Mr. Schoolcraft that it contained a message from the Indians to the President and the particulars of this message are fully set forth in his text. At first I doubted if the object could have any other purpose than a sacrificial one and was inclined to discredit the statement of the Moki interpreter. But on learning that the Navajo had a similar arrangement of sticks and feathers, which was called by the significant name of keçàn-yalçì', or talking kethàwn, I was more inclined to believe that some of these kethàwns may answer a double purpose and be used to convey messages, or at least serve as mnemonic aids to envoys.

180. The cac-bikeçàn (bear kethàwn) spoken of in the myth consisted of two sticks, each a span long, one painted black (male), the other painted blue (female). Each had red and blue bands at the ends and in the middle. There were no feathers or beads. (Paragraph 40.)

181. The glöï-bikeçàn, or sacrifices to the weasels, were four in number, two yellow and two white. In preparing the sticks one end was always to be held to the north, the other towards the south. At each end a narrow circle of red and a narrow circle of blue were painted; the red being to the north, i. e., outside of the blue at one end and inside of it at the other. The weasel men directed that the sticks should be buried in the ground in the same direction in which they were held when being made, lying from north to south with the outer red ring at the north. (Paragraph 41.)

182. Four sticks pertained to the klictsò-bikeçàn: one was black, with four white deer tracks painted on it; another was blue, with four yellow deer tracks; a third was white, with four black deer tracks; the fourth was yellow, with four blue deer tracks. The Great Serpent said to the Navajo prophet: "There are certain moles who, when they dig in the ground, scatter the earth in a long winding heap like the form of a crawling snake. In such a heap of earth will you bury these kethàwns." (Paragraph 42.)

183. There are two sticks belonging to the kethàwn of the lightning god (içnì'-bikeçàn). One is black, with a white zigzag stripe from end

to end; the other blue, with a yellow zigzag stripe from end to end. (Paragraph 43.)

184. The Estsàn-ɖigìni, or Holy Women, showed the prophet but one kethàwn stick. It was painted white and decorated with three pairs of circular bands, red and blue, the blue in each case being next to the body of the painter while he holds the stick in decorating it. This kethàwn must be buried at the base of a young spruce tree, with the first blue circle next to the tree. (Paragraph 45.)

185. Four sticks were shown by the Tcikè-cac-nátlehi. They were black, sprinkled with specular iron ore to make them shine; decorated with three pairs of bands, red and blue, applied as in the kethàwns of the Estsàn-ɖigìni; and buried under a young piñon, with the first blue band or circle next to the tree. (Paragraph 46.)

186. The two kethàwns seen by Dsilyi' Neyáni at Big Oaks, the home of the ɸigin-yosíni, were both banded at the ends with blue and red and had marks to symbolize the givers. One was white, with two pairs of stripes, red and blue, running lengthwise. The other was yellow, with many stripes of black and yellow running lengthwise. (Paragraph 49.)

187. At Last Mountain, the home of the skunks, two kethàwns, evidently intended to symbolize these animals, were shown to the prophet and his divine companions. Both the sticks were black: one had three white longitudinal stripes on one side; the other had three longitudinal rows of white spots, three spots in each row, on one side. (Paragraph 50.)

188. The two sticks shown by the squirrels, Glo'dsilkàï and Glo'dsiljíni, were painted blue, sprinkled with specular iron ore, and surrounded at the ends with red and blue bands. One was to be planted at the base of a pine tree and one at the base of a spruce tree.

189. At Dsilyà-içín the porcupines exhibited two kethàwns. They were very short, being equal in length to the middle joint of the little finger. One was black and one was blue. Each had red and blue terminal bands and each had a number of white dots on one side to represent porcupine quills. "Bury them," said ɸasàni, "under a piñon tree." (Paragraph 52.)

190. At Qoɸestsò four kethàwns, rather elaborately decorated, were shown. Two were half white and half black, the black part having white spots and the white part having black spots on it. The other two were half blue and half yellow, the yellow being spotted with blue and the blue with yellow. There were red and blue rings at the ends. (Paragraph 53.)

191. The Tçikè-ɖigìni showed their visitors two kethàwns, one black and one blue. Each was a span long and was surrounded with three pairs of bands, blue and red, put on in the manner observed in making the kethàwns of the Estsàn-ɖigìni. (Paragraph 184.) To the center of the black kethàwn five blue feathers were tied. To the center of the

blue ketháwn five yellow feathers were fastened. Five black beads were interred with the black stick — one tied to the center, one stuck in the end, and three laid loose in the ground. Five blue turquoise beads were similarly buried with the blue stick. Such ketháwns must be buried at the foot of a spruce tree, with the heads towards the mountains of Çepéntsa. By "head" is meant the end held the farther from the body of the painter when the paint is applied, the end having the red band at its extremity. (Paragraph 54.)

ORIGINAL TEXTS AND TRANSLATIONS OF SONGS, &C.

192. The songs of the dsilyídje qaçàl are very numerous and their recitation is governed by many rules, a few of which only have been discovered by the writer.

193. A list has been recorded of thirteen sets of songs which may properly be sung at night in the medicine lodge, when the ceremonies of the day are done, and in the corral on the last night, when there is no special song in progress pertaining to a particular alili or dance. The list which follows exhibits the order in which these songs may be sung on any particular night. For example, if the singers begin with a song from set III, they cannot follow immediately with a song from sets I or II, but must select from some of the following sets, as set IV or V. Again, in each set the songs have a certain order of sequence which must not be reversed. For convenience these will be called

SONGS OF SEQUENCE.

Order.	Indian name of set.	English name of set.	Number in each set.
I.	Atsáleï Bigin	Songs of the First Dancers	16
II.	Tsintsò Bigin	Songs of the Great Stick, or Plumed Wand	12
III.	Çepè Bigin	Songs of the Mountain Sheep	12
IV.	I'çnï' Bigin	Songs of the Lightning	12
V.	Tsilkè-çigìni Bigin	Songs of the Holy Young Men	12
VI.	Tcikè-cac-nátlehi Bigin	Songs of Young Women Who Become Bears	16
VII.	Dsilyi' Neyáni Bigin	Songs of Reared Within the Mountains	8
VIII.	Tsáhagin	Awl songs	8
IX.	Nahikàï-gin	Whitening songs	8
X.	Çasàni Bigin	Songs of the Porcupines	7
XI.	Nanisè Bigin	Songs of the Plants	8
XII.	Tsinçilçòï Bigin	Songs of the Exploding Stick	26
XIII.	Yikàï-gin	Daylight songs	16
	Total		161

194. Besides those referred to in the above list, there are more which are appropriate to different acts in the ceremony, such as the songs sung at the obliteration of the pictures, at the building of the corral, at the departure of the akáninili, &c.

195. In some cases a number of songs in the same set are nearly alike ; the addition or substitution of one verse, or even of one word, may be the only difference. Such songs usually follow one another in immediate succession ; often, on the other hand, we find a great variety in subject and in style.

196. Some songs are self-explanatory or readily understood, but the greater number cannot be comprehended without a full knowledge of the mythology and of the symbolism to which they refer; they merely hint at mythic conceptions. Many contain archaic expressions, for which the shaman can assign a meaning, but whose etymology cannot now be learned; and some embody obsolete words whose meaning is lost even to the priesthood. There are many vocables known to be meaningless and recited merely to fill out the rhythm or to give a dignified length to the song. For the same reasons a meaningless syllable is often added or a significant syllable duplicated.

197. Other poetical licenses are taken, such as the omission of a syllable, the change of accent, the substitution of one vowel for another. The most familiar words are often distorted beyond recognition. For these various reasons the task of noting and translating these songs is one of considerable difficulty.

198. FIRST SONG OF THE FIRST DANCERS.

Qaniè qaò yaè, qaniè qaò yaè
Qaniè iè oayè oayè.

1. Qadjináïa qaò yaè,
2. Kaç dsil ḍilhyíli qaò yaè,
3. 'Çaltsoï tseë qaò yaè,
4. Cija cigèlgo qaò yaè.
    Náhi ìni èhi oayè, náhi ìni èhi oöhè.

5. Niqoyastcàdje qaò yaè,
6. Kaç dsil çolíji qaò yaè,
7. Kini bitsèë qaò yaè,
8. Cija cigèlgo qaò yaè.
    Náhi ìni, etc.

9. Qadjináïa qaò yaè,
10. Kaç dsil litsòï qaò yaè,
11. Bitselitsòï qaò yaè,
12. Cija cigèlgo qaò yaè.
    Náhi ìni, etc.

13. Niqoyastcàdje qaò yaè,
14. Kaç dsil lakàie qaò yaè,
15. A'a'i tsèe qaò yaè,
16. Cija cigèlgo qaò yaè.
    Náhi ìni, etc.

199. *Translation.*—1, 9. Qadjináï, "Place-where-they-came-up," a locality in the San Juan Mountains where, according to their mythology, the Navajo emerged from the lower world to this. 5, 13. Niqoyastcàdje, another name for Qadjináï. 2, 6, 10, 14. Kaç, now ; dsil, mountain ; ḍilhyíli, black ; çolíji, blue ; litsòï, yellow ; lakàie, white. These verses refer to four mountains surrounding Qadjináï, which are designated by colors only to indicate their topographical positions. 3, 7, 11, 15. 'Çaltsoï= aça litsòï, "yellow wing," a large bird of prey ; kini, hen hawk ; bitselitsòï, "yellow tail," a bird of undetermined species ; a'a'i, magpie ; tse, a tail ; bitse, its tail. 4, 8, 12, 16. Cija, my treasure ; cigèl, my desideratum, my ultimatum, the only thing I

will accept. When supposed to be said by a god, as in this song, it means the particular sacrifice which is appropriate to him. In this case probably the feathers spoken of are "cigèl" and the mountains "cija." The refrain "qaò yaè" is a poetic modification of qaa', ịt looms up, or sticks up, said of some lofty object visible in the distance, whose base cannot be seen.

200. *Free translation.*

Place-whence-they-came-up looms up,
Now the black mountain looms up,
The tail of the "yellow wing" looms up,
My treasure, my sacrifice, loom up.

Land-where-they-moved-out looms up,
Now the blue mountain looms up,
The tail of the hen-hawk looms up,
My treasure, my sacrifice, loom up.

Place-whence-they-came-up looms up,
Now the yellow mountain looms up,
The tail that is yellow looms up,
My treasure, my sacrifice, loom up.

Land-where-they-moved-out looms up,
Now the white mountain looms up,
The tail of the magpie looms up,
My treasure, my sacrifice, loom up.

201. FIRST SONG OF THE MOUNTAIN SHEEP.

1. Yìki ȼasizìni,
2. Kaç Tsilkè-ȼigìni,
3. Kaç kátso-yisçàni,
4. Tsíȼa baällli,
5. Bíja-yeȼigíngo.

6. Kaç Tcikè ȼigìui,
7. Kátsoye yisçàni,
8. Yìki ȼasizìni,
9. Tsíȼa baällli,
10. Bíja-yeȼigíngo.

202. *Translation.*—1, 8. Yìki, upon it; ȼasizin, he stands on high. 2, 6. Kaç, now; tsilkè, young man; tcikè, young woman; ȼigìni, holy. 3. Kátso-yisçàn, the great plumed arrow; kátsoye yisçàn, with the great plumed arrow. 4, 9. Tsíȼa, truly, verily; baällli, an alili, a show, a rite, or implement used in a dance for him. 5, 10. Bíja, his treasure, his special property, his peculiar belonging; ye, with, a prefix forming nouns which denote the means; ȼigíngo, positively holy or supernatural. Bíja-yeȼigíngo might be translated "charm" or "talisman."

203. *Free translation.*

He stands high upon it;
Now the Holy Young Man [Young Woman,
   in second stanza],
With the great plumed arrow,

Verily his own sacred implement,
His treasure, by virtue of which he is truly
holy.

204. A reference to the myth and the description of the ceremonies will probably be sufficient to give the reader an understanding of this song. This set of songs, it is said, was first sung by the black sheep which stood on the rock as a sign to the Navajo fugitive; hence the name. (See paragraphs 35, 47, 48, 54.)

205. SIXTH SONG OF THE MOUNTAIN SHEEP.

Binaçoöláe [four times] oäyèhe oöhè.

1. Kaç Tsilkè-ȼigìni,
2. Ca'bitlòli yèë,
3. Tsíȼa biallli,
4. Bíja yeȼigíngo,
5. Binaçoöláe oäyèhe oöhè.

6. Kaç Tcikè-ȼigìni,
7. Natsilíçi yèë,
8. Tsíȼa biallli,
9. Bíja yeȼigíngo,
10. Binaçoöláe oäyèhe oöhè.

206. *Translation.*— 1, 6. Kaç, now; tsilkè, young man; tcikè, young woman; ɖigìni, holy one, god or goddess. 2. Ca'bitlòl, sunbeam, sunbeams; ye, with. 3, 8. Tsíɸa, verily; birJìli (paragraph 3), his dance or sacred implement. 4, 9. Bíja, his special property, his treasure; yeɖigíngo, that by means of which he is ɖigín, i. e., holy or supernatural. 5, 10. Binaɔòla, it is encircled. 7. Natsiliç, the rainbow.

207. *Free translation.*

Now the Holy Young Man,
With the sunbeam,
Verily his own sacred implement,
His treasure which makes him holy,
Is encircled.

Now the Holy Young Woman,
With the rainbow,
Verily her own sacred implement,
Her treasure which makes her holy,
Is encircled.

208. Which is to say that the great plumed arrows which they bear are adorned with sunbeams and rainbows. They "shine in glory." (See references in paragraph 204.)

209. TWELFTH SONG OF THE MOUNTAIN SHEEP.

1. Nayunáni tcènia,
2. Kaç biçèïltsos tcènia,
3. Biqolçègo, tcènia.

4. Nayunáni tcènia,
5. Kaç biçènackòji tcènia,
6. Biqolçègo, tcènia.

210. *Translation.*—1, 4. Nayunáni, again on the other side, i. e., across two valleys. 2. Biçè, his horns; iltsos, slender; biçèïltsos, slender horns, i. e., the deer, by metonomy. 3, 6. Biqolçègo, it is becoming to him. 5. Biçè, his horns; nackòj, turgid, filled out, stuffed; biçènackòji, turgid horns—metonymically, the mountain sheep, *Ovis montana.* The refrain, tcènia, he appears, he comes in sight.

211. *Free translation.*

Far beyond he appears;
Now "Slender Horn" appears.
His antlers are becoming. He appears.

Far beyond he appears;
Now "Turgid Horn" appears.
His horns are becoming. He appears.

212. This song, it is said, refers to the time when the prophet saw the vision of the black sheep on the rock. (Paragraph 35.) The reason for introducing the deer into the song is not obvious.

213. FIRST SONG OF THE THUNDER.

1. Çòna! Çòna! A'āīyèhe oöhè [repeat],
2. Yùçakoö ani';
3. I'ɖni'djiè ani';
4. Kos ɖilhyíl biyì'dje,
5. Nàbizaç qolègo,
6. Çòna! Çòna! A'āīyèhe oöhè.

7. Çòna! Çòna! A'āīyèhe oöhè [repeat],
8. Yùyakoö ani';
9. Anilçàni ani';
10. Nánise biçqàko,
11. Nàbizaç qolègo,
12. Çòna ! Çòna! A'āīyèhe oöhè.

214. *Translation.*— 1, 6, 7, 12. Çòna, an imitation of the thunder, not a word. 2, 8. Yùçako, above; yùyako, below; ani', any sound, the sound of the voice. 3. I'ɖni'dji, pertaining to the thunder. 4. Kos, cloud; ɖilhyíl, black, dark; biyì'dje, within, or toward within it. 5, 11. Nàbizaç qolègo, again and again sounds his moving voice. 9. Anilçàni, a general name for large meadow grasshoppers.—10. Nánise, plants in general; biçqàko, in among them.

215. *Free translation.*

Thonah! Thonah!
There is a voice above,
The voice of the thunder.
Within the dark cloud,
Again and again it sounds,
Thonah! Thonah!

Thonah! Thonah!
There is a voice below,
The voice of the grasshopper.
Among the plants,
Again and again it sounds,
Thonah! Thonah!

216. TWELFTH SONG OF THE THUNDER.

Aïena.
Beqojònigo ani'i [four times] oöhè.

1. Yùçakoö ani'i;
2. I'ǫni'djië ani'i;
3. Kos ǫilhyíl biyì'dje,
4. Nàbizaç qolègo,
5. Beqojònigo ani'i, oöhè.

6. Yùyakoö ani'i;
7. Anilçàni ani'i;
8. Nánise biçqàko,
9. Nàbizaç qolègo,
10. Beqojònigo ani'i, oöhè.

217. *Translation.*—Aïena, a meaningless beginning to many songs, which may be omitted. 1. Yùçako, above. 2. I'ǫni'dji, pertaining to the thunder. 3. Kos, cloud; ǫilhyíl, dark; biyì'dje, within it. 4, 9. Nàbizaç, his voice again, his voice repeated; qolègo, sounds along, sounds moving. 5, 10. (Be, a prefix forming nouns of the cause or instrument; qojòni, local or terrestrial beauty; go, a suffix to qualifying words); beqojònigo, productive of terrestrial beauty; ani', a voice, a sound. 6. Yùyako, below. 7. Anilçàni, grasshopper. 8. Nánise, plants; biçqàko, in among them.

218. *Free translation.*

The voice that beautifies the land!
The voice above,
The voice of the thunder
Within the dark cloud
Again and again it sounds,
The voice that beautifies the land.

The voice that beautifies the land!
The voice below;
The voice of the grasshopper
Among the plants
Again and again it sounds,
The voice that beautifies the land.

219. FIRST SONG OF THE HOLY YOUNG MEN, OR YOUNG MEN GODS.

1. Oöc 'çqa nagäïë,
2. Kaç Tsilkè-ǫigìni,
3. Dsil ǫilhyíl biyàgi,
4. Biyàji naïlè.

5. Aie 'çqa nagäïë,
6. Kaç Tcikè-ǫigìni,
7. Dsil çolíj biyàgi,
8. Biyàji naïlè.

220. *Translation.*—1, 5. 'Çqa=biçqa, amid or among them; nagai, that, there. 2. Kaç, now; Tsilkè-ǫigìni, Holy Young Man; Tcikè-ǫigìni, Holy Young Woman. 3, 7. Dsil, mountain; ǫilhyíl, black; çolíj, blue; biyàgi, at the foot of, at the base of. 4, 8. Biyàji, his child; naïlè, he lays down, he leaves.

221. *Free translation.*

There amid [the mountains],
Now the Holy Young Man,
At the foot of the black mountain,
Lays down his child.

There amid [the mountains],
Now the Holy Young Woman,
At the foot of the blue mountain,
Lays down her child.

222. The characters of Tsilkè-ǫigìni and Tcikè-ǫigìni are in the myth. The black mountain pertains to the male, the blue to the female. Although not told with the rest of the myth, it was subsequently related to the writer that Tsilkè-ǫigìni said to the prophet, " Whoever learns

our songs will thenceforth be our child." The above song, it is said, has some reference to this promise; but a fuller explanation, no doubt, remains to be discovered.

223. SIXTH SONG OF THE HOLY YOUNG MEN.

Aïena.
Altsàcië ɕigìni oöhè.

1. Altsàcië ɕigìni, altsàcië ɕigìni, altsàcië ɕigìni oöhè.
2. Kaç Tsilkè-ɕigìni, bakàgië ɕigìni,
3. Dsil ɕilhyíli eë, bakàgië ɕigìni,
4. Tsìntsoï ɕilhyíli e bakàgië ɕigìni,
5. Tsíɕa bialìli, bíja yeɕigíngo, bakàgië ɕigìni, oöhè.

Altsàcië ɕigìni oöhè.

6. Altsàcië ɕigìni, altsàcië cigìni, altsàcië ɕigìni oöhè.
7. Kaç Tcikè-ɕigìni, bakàgië ɕigìni,
8. Dsil çolíji eë, bakàgië ɕigìni,
9. Tsìntsoï çolíji, bakàgië ɕigìni,
10. Tsíɕa bialìli, bíja yeɕigíngo, bakàgië cigìni, oöhè.

224. *Translation.*—1, 6. Altsàcië, on each side; ɕigìni, a holy one, a god. 2, 7. Kaç, now; tsilkè, young man; tcikè, young woman; bakàgi, on the summit, on top of it. 3, 8. Dsil, mountain; ɕilhyíl, dark, black; çolíj, blue. 4, 9. Tsìntsoï, great stick, a notched stick used as a musical instrument in the dance. 5, 10. Tsíɕa bialìli, truly his dance implement; bíja yeɕigíngo, his holy treasure, his talisman, his charm, his magic wand.

225. *Free translation.*

There's a god on each side.
Now the Holy Young Man
Is the god on top of the black mountain,
With his black notched stick,
The implement of his dance, his magic wand.

There's a god on each side.
Now the Holy Young Woman
Is the god on top of the blue mountain,
With her blue notched stick,
The implement of her dance, her magic wand.

226. This song is said to refer to that part of the myth where it is related that the prophet, flying from the Ute, climbed a hill which was transformed into a mountain. (Paragraph 38.) Each mountain was supposed to have a holy one on it, who could, by means of his notched stick, produce the metamorphosis. The mountains were not necessarily colored black and blue, but are thus described to indicate that they lay north and south of the prophet's path. (Paragraph 171.)

227. TWELFTH SONG OF THE HOLY YOUNG MEN.

Eäièa qàla éla yainàhe, oöhè.
Eäièa qàla éla yainooò yaaà yooò [three times],
Eäièa qàla éla yainà, qàla éla qainàhe oöhè.

1. Dsil ilhyíli inlòooò yaaà yooò,
2. Tsìntsoï ɕilhyíli inlòooò yaaà yeɕè.
3. Ci cigèlgo yainà,
    Qàla éla qainàhe oöhè.

4. Dsil çolíji inlòooò yaaà yooò,
5. Tsìntsoï çolíji inlòooò yaaà yeeè,
6. Ci cigèlgo yainà,
    Qàla éla qainàhe oöhè.

228. *Translation.*—1, 4. Dsil, mountain; ɕilhyíl, black; çolíj, blue. 2, 5. Tsìntsò, a notched stick used in ceremonies to make music; inlo (inla'), they lie there (two long hard things lie). 3, 6. Cigèl, my ultimatum, my desideratum (said of the peculiar sacrifice which belongs to each god), something I (the god) will have and accept nothing in place of it, my special sacrifice.

229. *Free translation.*

There lie the black mountains:	There lie the blue mountains;
There lie the black sticks;	There lie the blue sticks;
There lie my sacrifices.	There lie my sacrifices.

230. This is supposed to be a part of the instructions which the Holy Young Men and Holy Young Women gave to the prophet. The tsintso is made of cherry, which grows only on high mountains in the Navajo country. The sticks are painted black and blue. (See paragraph 171.) The song alludes to all these facts.

231. EIGHTH SONG OF THE YOUNG WOMEN WHO BECOME BEARS.

Ço¢ig̣iniȼa oyàhe oöhè,
Ço¢ig̣iniȼa oyà oyà ooyàya
   Hāiyàya hāiyàya hāiyàhe, oöhè.
1. Kaȼ Tsilkè-¢ig̣inië ço¢ig̣inȼa hāiyàhe,
   oöhè,
2. Bitsintsòië ië ço¢ig̣inȼa hāiyàhe oöhè,
3. Tsíȼa biall:lië bíja-ye¢ig̣inië, oyà oyà,
   oyàya,
   Hāiyàya hāiyàya hāiyàhe, oöhè.

Ço¢ig̣iniȼa oyàhe, oöhè,
Ço¢ig̣iniȼa oyà oyà ooyàya,
   Hāiyàya hāiyàya hāiyàhe, oöhè.
4. Kaȼ Tcikè-¢ig̣inië ço¢ig̣inȼa hāiyàhe,
   oöhè,
5. Bitsintsòië ië ço¢ig̣inȼa hāiyàhe oöhè,
6. Tsíȼa biallïlië bíja-ye¢ig̣inië, oyà oyà,
   oyàya,
   Hāiyàya hāiyàya hāiyàhe, oöhè.

232. *Translation.*—Ço¢ig̣iniȼa, ço¢ig̣inȼa, he is not a god; it is not holy; it is not divine. 1, 4. Kaȼ, now; tsilkè, young man; tcikè, young woman; ¢ig̣ini, holy, supernatural. 2, 4. Bitsintsòi, his great notched stick. 3, 6. Tsíȼa, verily; biallli, his implement of the dance or rite; bíja-ye¢ig̣ini, his treasure which makes holy; his magic wand.

233. *Free translation.*

The Holy Young Man is not divine;	The Holy Young Woman is not divine;
His great notched stick is not holy;	Her great notched stick is not holy;
His magic wand is not holy.	Her magic wand is not holy.

234. This is supposed to refer to an altercation between these two gods, in which they tried to belittle each other.

235. I have another song of this series, in which the idea is conveyed that their powers depend on their magic wands or notched sticks.

236. ONE OF THE AWL SONGS.

Òwe òwe òwe yàni yàï owà" na a [repeat three times],
Òwe òwe ïni áhe oöhè,

1. 'Ke-cac-natlèhi natcagàhi,
2. Kaȼ dsil ¢ilhyíli bakàgi natcagàhi,
3. Kaȼ ni‘ inzàȼ inȼì ¢oholniȼa òua,
4. Kaȼ ni‘ inzàȼ inȼì ¢oniòȼa òna.

5. Tcikè-¢ig̣ini natcagàhi,
6. Dsil ¢olíji bakàgi natcagàhi,
7. Kaȼ ni‘ inzàȼ inȼì, ¢oholniȼa òna,
8. Kaȼ ni‘ inzàȼ inȼì, ¢oniòȼa òna.

237. *Translation.*—1. Ke, an abbreviation of tcikè; Tcikè-cac-natlèhi, maiden who becomes a bear; natcagà‘, she travels far, she walks or wanders far around. 2. Kaȼ, now; dsil ¢ilhyíl, black mountain; bakàgi, on top of. 3, 4, 7, 8. Ni‘, earth, land; inzàȼ, distant; inȼì, it lies, it stretches; ¢oholniȼa, seems not to be; ¢oniòȼa, not obscure or dim like a faint distance. 6. Dsil ¢olíji bakàgi, on top of the blue mountains.

238. *Free translation.*

The Maid Who Becomes a Bear walks far around
On the black mountains, she walks far around.
Far spreads the land. It seems not far [to her].
Far spreads the land. It seems not dim [to her].

The Holy Young Woman walks far around
On the blue mountains, she walks far around.
Far spreads the land. It seems not far [to her].
Far spreads the land. It seems not dim [to her].

239. FIRST SONG OF THE EXPLODING STICK.

Aïena.

Aïeyà aïa aïeyà iè eè ieèe [three times] ië la^n.

1. 'Ke-cac-nátlèhi dsilyi' ¢i¢ílko^n ië na^n,
2. Dsilyi' ¢olkòlko^n; dsil beko^{n}nìçe ië na^n, Ië na^n yahà hāīà ië na^n aï.

3. Çabasçìni ço'yi' ¢i¢ílko^n ië na^n,
4. Ço'yi ¢olkòlko^n; ço'beko^{n}nìçe ië na^n, Ië na^n yahà hāīà ië na^n aï.

240. *Translation.*—1, 3. 'Ke-cac-natlèhi=Tcikè-cac-nátlehi, Young Woman Who Becomes a Bear; Çabasçin, the Otter; ¢i¢ílko^n, he or she set on fire in many places. 2, 4. Dsil, mountains; dsilyi', in the mountains; ço', water, waters; ço'yi', in the waters; ¢olkòlko^n, he set on fire as he went along; beko^{n}nìçe, its fires in a line, its string of fires.

241. *Free translation.*

Young Woman Who Becomes a Bear set fire in the mountains
In many places; as she journeyed on
There was a line of burning mountains.

The Otter set fire in the waters
In many places; as he journeyed on
There was a line of burning waters.

242. It is related that in the ancient days, during a year of great drought, these holy ones, on their way to a council of the gods, set fire to the mountains and the waters. The smoke arose in great clouds, from which rain descended on the parched land. The song alludes to this legend.

243. LAST SONG OF THE EXPLODING STICK.

Hiè ieeè naāīà āīà i a ai a^n a^u [twice] ie.

1. Tcikè-cac-náatlehië ¢igìni qayikàlgo; bàniya āīè.
2. Dsil aga ¢azàgië ¢igìni qayikàlgo; bàniya āīè.
3. Tsí¢a ci cigèliye ¢igìni qayikàlgo; bàniya āīè.
4. Yàne ¢oölànegoö ¢isitsaàye. Hiè ieeè naāīà, etc.

5. Kaç Tcikè ¢igìni ¢igìni qayikàlgo; bàniya āīè.
6. Kos aga ¢azàgiï ¢igìni qayikàlgo; bàniya āīè.
7. Tsí¢a ci cigèliye ¢igìni qayikàlgo; bàniya āīè.
8. Yàne ¢uöלànegoö ¢isitsaàye. Hiè ieeè naāīà, etc.

244. *Translation.*—1, 5. Tcikè-cac-náatlehi, Young Woman Who Becomes a Bear; Tcikè-¢igìni, Holy Young Woman, or young woman goddess; ¢igìni qayikàl, she journeyed seeking the gods; bàniya, she found them, she met them. 2, 6. Dsil, mountains; kos, clouds; aga, peak, summit; ¢azà', many pointing upwards; (dsil aga ¢azàgi, on many mountain peaks). 3, 7. Tsí¢a, truly or true; cigèl, my desideratum, my special sacrifice. 4, 8. Ç̸oölàne=¢oölà¢a, some one does not believe it; ¢isitsà, I have heard; yàne and other vocables are meaningless.

245. *Free translation.*

Maid Who Becomes a Bear sought the gods and found them;	Holy Young Woman sought the gods and found them;
On the high mountain peaks she sought the gods and found them;	On the summits of the clouds she sought the gods and found them;
Truly with my sacrifice she sought the gods and found them.	Truly with my sacrifice she sought the gods and found them.
Somebody doubts it, so I have heard.	Somebody doubts it, so I have heard.

246. These songs are accompanied, in beating the drum, with a peculiar sharp strike like a sudden outburst or explosion. Hence, they say, the name, Tsinȼilçöï Bigin.

247. FIRST DAYLIGHT SONG.

Çahizȼìle, çahizȼìle, ya ahāìà la^n [four times].

1. Kaç Yikāï-acikè çahizȼìle, ya ahāìà la^n,
2. Qaïyolkàlȼe çahizȼìle, ya ahāìà la^n,
3. Bitsídje yolkàlgo çahizȼìle, ya ahāìà la^n,
4. Bikècȼe yolkàlgo çahizȼìle, ya ahāìà la^n.
5. Bitsídje qojògo çahizȼìle, ya ahāìà la^n,
6. Bikècȼe qojògo çahizȼìle, ya ahāìà la^n,
7. Bizàçȼe qojògo çahizȼìle, ya ahāìà la^n.
   Çahizȼìle, çahizȼìle, etc.

8. Kaç yikāï-açèç, çahizȼìle, ya ahāìà la^n,
9. Naqotsòïȼe çahizȼìle, ya ahāìà la^n.
   [Verses 3 to 7 are here repeated.]
   Çahizȼìle, çahizȼìle, etc.

248. *Translation.*—Çahizȼìle=çahizȼel, it hangs as a curtain or festoon; it hangs supported at both ends, i. e., the white curtain of dawn so hangs. 1. Yikāï-acikè, the Daylight Boy, the Navajo dawn god. 2. Qayolkàlȼe, from the place of dawn. 3. Bitsídje, before him; yolkàlgo, as it dawns, as the night passes away. 4. Bikècȼe, from behind him. Qojògo, in a beautiful (earthly) manner. 7. Bizàçȼe, from his voice. 8. Yikāï-açèç, the Daylight Girl—the dawn goddess. 9. Naqotsòïȼe, from the land of yellow light (horizontal terrestrial yellow).

249. *Free translation.*

The curtain of daybreak is hanging,	Behind him, in beauty, it is hanging;
The Daylight Boy (it is hanging),	From his voice, in beauty, it is hanging.
From the land of day it is hanging;	
Before him, as it dawns, it is hanging;	The Daylight Girl (it is hanging),
Behind him, as it dawns, it is hanging.	From the land of yellow light, it is hanging, &c. (substituting her for him and his).
Before him, in beauty, it is hanging;	

250. LAST DAYLIGHT SONG.

Loleyèe, Loleyèe. Loleyèe, Loleyèe.
Loleyèe, Loleyèe. Yahāìee qanaāï.

1. Qayolkàgo, Loleyèe.
2. Kaç Yikāï-acikèe. Loleyèe.
   Loleyèe, Loleyèe. Yahāìèe, qanaāï.
3. Kaç aȼa yiskàgo. Loleyèe.
4. Kaç Yikāï-açèçe. Loleyèe.
   Loleyèe, Loleyèe. Yahāìee, qanaāï.

251. *Translation.*—1. Qayolkàgo, in the place of dawn. 2, 4. Yikāï-acikè and Yikāï-açèç, Daylight Boy and Daylight Girl (see paragraph 248). 3. Aȼa yiskàgo, it is day all around. Refrain, loleyè, lullaby, a meaningless expression to indicate sleepiness.

252. *Free translation.*

Lullaby, lullaby.	Now it is day. Lullaby.
It is daybreak. Lullaby.	Now comes the Daylight Girl. Lullaby.
Now comes the Daylight Boy. Lullaby.	

253. As the daylight songs are sung just at dawn, in the corral, before the dance ceases, their significance is apparent.

OTHER SONGS AND EXTRACTS.

254. SONG OF THE PROPHET TO THE SAN JUAN RIVER.

Aïena.

1. Nagāī ҫonilínië, nagāī ҫonilínië,
2. Biҫhyísgo cinì' ɖeyà'
   Haïniyèa, haïniyèa, āïèe niò haïneyàhe, oöhè.

3. Nagāī ҫointyèlië, nagāī ҫonilínië,

4. Biҫhyísgo cinì' ɖeyà'
   Haïniyèa, etc.

5. Nagāī saⁿ biҫòië, nagāī ҫonilínië,
6. Biҫhyísgo cinì' ɖeyà'
   Haïniyèa, etc.

255. *Translation.*—1. Nagāī, that; ҫonilíni, flowing water, a river. 2, 4, 6. Biҫhyísgo, across it; cinì', my mind; ɖeyà', it goes, or, it comes, it wanders to or from. 3. Ҫointyèli, broad water. 5. Saⁿ biҫo, water of old age.

256. For origin and free translation of this song, see paragraph 22.

257. SONG OF THE BUILDING OF THE DARK CIRCLE.

Oeà oeà, eà eà, he he ;
Oeà oeà, eà eeà, he he, ee naⁿ a.

1. Dsilyi' Neyáni, cayolèli cayolèli ;
2. Tcoyaj ɖilhyíli, cayolèli cayolèli ;
3. Tsíca alìli, cayolèli cayolèli ;
4. Bíja ɖigíngo, cayolèli cayolèli.

5. Tcikè-ɖigìni, cayolèli cayolèli ;
6. Tcoyaj ҫolíji, cayolèli cayolèli ;
7. Tsíɖa alìli, cayolèli cayolèli ;
8. Bíja cigíugo, cayolèli cayolèli.

258. *Translation.*—1. Dsilyi' Neyáni, Reared Within the Mountains, the prophet who instituted these ceremonies ; cayolèli, he carries [something long and flexible, as a branch or sapling] for me. 2, 6. Tcoyaj, a spruce sapling, diminutive of tco, spruce ; ɖilhyíl, black ; ҫolíj, blue. 3, 7. Tsíɖa alìli (usually tsíɖa bialìli), truly a dance implement. 4, 8. Bíja ɖigíngo (usually bíja-yeɖigíngo), a holy treasure, a magic wand.

259. *Free translation.*

Reared Within the Mountains carries for me ;
A black spruce sapling, he carries for me ;
An implement of the rites, he carries for me;
A holy treasure, he carries for me.

The Holy Young Woman carries for me ;
A blue spruce sapling, she carries for me ;
An implement of the rites, she carries for me ;
A holy treasure, she carries for me.

260. The evergreen poles used in the dance and in making the "dark circles," to both of which this song probably refers, were, in all cases where I have observed them, made of piñon and not of spruce ; but all dances I have witnessed were at altitudes of about six thousand feet, where piñon was abundant and spruce rare. In those portions of the Navajo country with which I am familiar the spruce (*Pseudotsuga douglassii*) grows plentifully at the height of eight thousand feet, sparsely below that. There is good reason for believing that the spruce is the true sacred tree of these rites and that the piñon is only a convenient substitute. The song is called Ilnásjin Beniҫà, "that with which the dark circle is built." It is sung by the shaman at the eastern gate, while the young men are building the corral. (Paragraph 124.) I have other

slightly different versions of it, probably suitable for different occasions. The form given above is recited, under ordinary circumstances, when the patient is a woman.

261. PRAYER TO DSILYI' NEYÁNI.

1. Dsilyi' Neyáni!
2. Dsil banaçà!
3. Tsilkè!
4. Naçàni!
5. Nigèl icla'.
6. Na¢è hila'.
7. Cikè caä¢ilil.
8. Citcàç caä¢ilil.
9. Citsès caä¢ilil.
10. Cinì' caä¢ilil.
11. Cinè caä¢ilil.
12. Qojògo qaçàlçe aci¢ilil.
13. Citsídje qojolel.
14. Cikè¢e qojolel.
15. Cizàç qaqojolel.
16. Qojòni qaslè,
17. Qojòni qaslè,
18. Qojòni qaslè,
19. Qojòni qaslè.

262. *Translation.*—1. The name of the prophet. 2. Dsil, mountains, banaçà, chief (or master) for them. 3. Tsilkè, young man. 4. Naçàni, chieftain. 5. Nigèl, your peculiar sacrifice, i. e., the keçàn; icla', I have made. 6. Na¢è, a smoke, i. e., the cigarettes (paragraph 87), for you; hila', is made. 7, 8, 9, 10, 11. Cikè, my feet; citcàç, my lower extremities; citsès, my body; cinì', my mind; cinè, my voice; caä¢ilil, for me restore (as it was before) thou wilt. 12. Qojògo, in a beautiful manner; qa¢àlçe, repaired, mended; aci¢ilil, restore me thou wilt. 13, 14. Citsídje, in the direction before me; cikè¢e, from behind me; qojolel, wilt thou terrestrially beautify. 15. Cizàç, my words; qaqojolel, wilt thou personally beautify. 16, 17, 18, 19. Qojòni, in earthly beauty; qaslè, it is made, it is done.

263. In other prayers, closely resembling this in form, the shaman adds : " Beautify all that is above me. Beautify all that is below me. Beautify all things around me."

264. The division into verses is that of the chanter. He pronounces the name in the first line; the patient repeats it after him. Then he gives out the words in the second line, and so on. For free translation, see paragraph 88.

265. SONG OF THE RISING SUN DANCE.

Oöniyàye, oöniyàye oöniyàhe
yáhe yáhe heyiyoè [twice].

1. Qanaïçácçe
2. Tsilkè-¢igìni
3. Kátso-yisçàni
4. Yìyolnakòe
5. Qano qakòsko.
6. Tcihanoàïe
7. Akos nisínle.
   Yáhe, yáhe eïa äï.

Oöniyàye, etc.

8. Inaïçácçe
9. Tcikè-¢igìni
10. Awètsal-yisçàni
11. Yìyolnakòe
12. Qana qokòsko.
13. Klehanoàïe
14. Akos nisínle.
    Yáhe, yáhe eïa äï.

266. *Translation.*—1. Qanaïçácçe, from where it (the sun) rises. 2. Tsilkè-¢igìni, Holy Young Man. 3. Kátso-yisçàni, the great plumed arrow. 4, 11. Yiyolna', he swallowed slowly or continuously. 5, 12. Qano qakòsko, it comes out by degrees. 6. Tcihanoàï, the sun. 7, 14. Akos nisín, he is satisfied. 8. Inaïçácçe, from where it sets. 9. Tcikè-¢igìni, Holy Young Woman. 10. Awètsal-yisçàni, prepared or plumed cliff rose, i. e., cliff rose arrow. 13. Klehanoàï, the moon.

5 ETH——30

267. *Free translation.*

Where the sun rises,	Where the sun sets,
The Holy Young Man	The Holy Young Woman
The great plumed arrow	The cliff rose arrow
Has swallowed	Has swallowed
And withdrawn it.	And withdrawn it.
The sun	The moon
Is satisfied.	Is satisfied.

268. This song is sung during the dance or alil described in para
graph 142. The conception of the poet seems to be that, the dance of
the great plumed arrow having been properly performed, the sun
should be satisfied and willing to do the bidding of the dancers, i. e.,
rise when desired, on the pole.

269. INSTRUCTIONS GIVEN TO THE AKÁNINILI.

1. Çi' betcána nilìⁿlel.
2. Çi' ¢a'naniltyèl¢o.
3. Çi' beniqo¢ílsinlel. Aïbinìgi nizè ¢ela'.
4. Ȼa'yiltsísgo, ¢a'bokògo tse'na akàn hyis¢inìle.

5. Tsiⁿ etlol akàn bàçhyis hyis¢inìle ; ako bàçhyis hyis¢ilçále.
6. Tse' elkàgi akàn hyis¢inìle.
7. Akoï kátso-yisçàn ; aïbinigi djoçile, qo¢igínçe behoèqo¢ilsin.

270. *Translation.*—1. Çi', this; betcáua, a thing to rise with (as you progress); nilìⁿlel, will make for you. 2. Çi', this; ¢a'naniltyèl¢o, will carry you along anywhere.
3. Beniqo¢ílsinlel, by means of it people will know you; aïbinigi, for this reason, or
purpose; nizè, your neck; ¢ela', it hangs (once) around. 4. Ȼa'yiltsísgo, at any little
valley (yiltsis, a little valley); ¢a'bokògo, at any gully or arroyo (boko', arroyo);
tse'na, across; akàn, meal; hyis¢inìle, he sprinkles always across. 5. Tsiⁿ etlol, the
root of a tree; akàn, meal; bàçhyis, across it; hyis¢inìle, he sprinkles across; ako,
then; hyis¢ilçále, he steps across. 6. Tse' elkàgi, on flat rocks; akàn, meal; hyis-
¢inìle, he sprinkles across. 7. Akoï, then, next; kátso-yisçàn, the great prepared
arrow—so says the chanter, but he really refers to the in¢ia', or çobolçà, the plumed
wand which akáninili carries; aïbinigi, for this purpose; djoçile, he carries it (in the
hand); qo¢igínçe, from a holy place (cigin, holy); behoèqo¢ilsin, by means of it
people know him.

271. For free translation, see paragraph 102.

272. PRAYER OF THE PROPHET TO HIS MASK.

1. Ȼa'andje qaha.,dsìgo ançèlini, cilìⁿ.
2. Hyininàleni, cilìⁿ.

3. Ayàⁿ¢aⁿ çocisyi'go¢olèléa, cilìⁿ.
4. Caï¢inilìl.

273. *Translation.*—1. Ȼa'andje, at any time to you; qahasdsìgo, when I spoke; ançèlini, always you made or did it, i. e., granted my request or assisted me; cilìⁿ, my
domestic animal, my pet. 2. Hyininàleni, you were alive (once); cilìⁿ, my pet.
3. Ayàⁿ¢aⁿ, be sure, take care; ço¢a, negative; cisyi'go, that I die; ¢olèl, I desire,
I beg (the divided negative makes one word of the sentence). 4. Caï¢inilìl, watch
thou for me, or over me.

274. For free translation, see paragraph 27.

275. LAST WORDS OF THE PROPHET.

1. Aqalàui, citsíli.
2. Cakaïlçe ye qoçigínçe.
3. Ǫa‘çonasiçilsèlça.
4. Ǫa‘hoelçìgo ça‘çeltcílgo, nagāïga cinàï aùila dsinisínle,

5. Ǫa‘no‘çílgo ayàc inçiçalàgo, anilçàni inçiçalàgo nagāïga cinàï binibikègola‘ dsinisínle.

276. *Translation.*—1. Aqalàni, greeting (farewell, in this case); citsíli, my younger brother. 2. Cakaïlçe, for me they have come; ye, the yays, the gods; qoçigínçe, from a holy or supernatural place. 3. (Ǫa‘, any, on any occasion, etc.; çoça, negative; na, again; siçilsèl, you will see me); ça‘çonasiçilsèlça, you will never see me again. 4. Ǫa‘hoelçìgo, on any occasion as the rain passes, i. e., whenever it rains; ça‘çeltcílgo, whenever it thunders; nagāïga, in that; cinàï, my elder brother; anìla, is his voice; dsinisínle, you will think so. 5. Ǫa‘no‘çílgo, whenever they (crops) are ripening, i. e., in harvest time; ayàc, small birds; inçiçalàgo, of all kinds; anilçàni, grasshoppers; nagāïga, in that, in those; cinàï, my elder brother; binibikègola‘, is his ordering, his design (the trail of his mind); dsinisínle, so you will think.

277. For free translation, see paragraph 79.

ADDENDUM

THE SUPPRESSED SECTIONS FROM THE 1884

EDITION OF *THE MOUNTAIN CHANT*

The following two sections were intended for inclusion in the 1883–84 edition of *The Mountain Chant* (Bureau of Ethnology, Fifth Annual Report, 1888), but were excised prior to publication. They later appeared in a five-page pamphlet, apparently self-published, entitled "The Suppressed Part of 'The Mountain Chant: A Navajo Ceremony,' by Dr. Washington Matthews, U.S.A. Extracted from the Fifth Annual Report of the Bureau of Ethnology, Washington, D.C., 1888." Fort Wingate, New Mexico. Feb. 26, 1892.

A notice in the front matter reprints paragraph 146 from *The Mountain Chant* and adds: "The present pamphlet contains the information suppressed in the original. The author begs the pardon of his correspondents for having so long delayed the fulfillment of his promise."

See Foreword, this volume p. xix, and Robert Poor, *Washington Matthews: An Intellectual Biography*, M.A. Thesis, University of Nevada, Reno, 37, 122–26.

THE PUBLISHER

After paragraph 130 of "The Mountain Chant," read the following:

While the dancers are circling around the fire in the dance of Nahikai, if one is found in a stooping or kneeling attitude before the fire, trying to burn the down on his want, another may come up from behind him, mount him and imitate, without actual pederasty, the pederastic motions of an erotic dog. While thus engaged a third dancer may mount the second and a fourth may mount the third and enact a like play—just as a number of dogs are often seen engaged.

Sometimes one or more of the actors wear large imitation penes, made of rags or inflated sheep-gut; such may enact the part of dogs, feign to masturbate or to manipulate the part to produce erection.

Sometimes, when the down has been burned from the wand and before it has been restored, they treat the wand as if it were a penis; hold it erect or semi-erect between the thighs, rub it and manipulate it. This is done mostly by the last remaining dancers, who effect to have difficulty in restoring the down to the ends of their wands.

Their motions are of such a nature that many white spectators of this play have conjectured that the dance of Nahikai is symbolic of the sexual act; that the down on the wand represents the desire which is destroyed in the flame of gratification, and, with trouble, restored; and this seems not an unreasonable conjecture.

After paragraph 145 of "The Mountain Chant," read the following:

That portion of the drama which succeeds the finding of the hoshkawn or yucca, I have seen enacted with varying detail and dialogue, but with the essential parts always similar. To preserve the unity, I will describe it as seen on the night of November 5th, 1882. (See "Mountain Chant," par. 127.)

DRAMATIS PERSONAE. —The old hunter and the man dressed as a woman, who will be referred to as He and She.

He. —Come, my wife, I have found something good. This is what I have looked for. Are you not glad I have found it?

She. —Yes, I am very glad, my sweet.

He. —It tastes like you. (He gives her a piece to eat.)

She. —It is sweet, but not as sweet as you.

(After this compliment he draws close to her and begins to dally, not over decently. One act is to put his hand under her clothes, withdraw it and smell it. At length he puts his hand in at the neck of her dress as if to feel her bosom and draws forth a handkerchief hidden there. He become furious.)

He (Squealing in feeble wrath). —Where did you get this?

She. —My aunt lost it at the spring and, when I went for water, I found it there.

He. —I don't believe you! You have been cohabiting with someone else. This is your pay.

She. —No, truly, my aunt lost it.

He (Still in a jealous fury, lights a cigarette and tries to smoke, presently throws cigarette peevishly away). —I will go away and never see you again.

She. —Don't leave! Don't Leave! You are a fool!

He. —Yes, I know it; but I will be one no longer. Now I go away. (He moves off.)

She. (Pouts a moment, then takes a pinch of dust in her fingers, blows it toward him and says:) —Thus do I blow away my regard for you. I will follow you no more.

(With head averted, and sitting, she watches him furtively till he shuffles off out of sight, among the crowd of spectators; then she runs after him and soon reappears dragging him back.)

He. —You were not strong enough to blow me away, I am so sweet. (Again they sit side by side and indulge in dalliance and loud kisses).

He. —I don't like you to cohabit with others while I am away hunting. I find you food and sweet things to eat, but you are bad.

She. —Do not leave me. I will never touch another man again. (They eat together of the yucca fruit.)

He. —How sweet this fruit is! Let us see which is the sweeter, this or coition. (Each puts a piece in the mouth and they proceed with the most complete realism of action, but without exposure, to imitate the sexual act. When through, he tumbles off with a groan as if completely exhausted.)

She (Spitting the fruit form her mouth). —The hoshkawn is sweet, but not half so sweet as what we have been doing. (She rises, takes a handful of dust from the ground, and acts as if scattering it on the vulva. They put the fruit into a basket and depart.)

The spectators of this scene are persons of both sexes—married and unmarried—and of all ages; a most promiscuous audience.

The act of dusting the vulva I have heard of as done by Indian women of other tribes in the arid region after the act of coition *al fresco.*

The dialogue given above was obtained for me by Mr. A. M. Stephen of Keam's Canyon, Arizona, who witnessed with me the night ceremonies of November 5th, 1882, and next day, learned the words of the play from the man who enacted the part of the woman. I have since heard other versions of the dialogue, but none superior to this.

W. M.